D1161483

War and Peace

War and Peace

Discovering Mythology

**Other titles in Lucent Books
Discovering Mythology series include:**

War and Peace

Discovering Mythology

by Susan Glick

LUCENT BOOKS®

THOMSON

™

GALE

San Diego • Detroit • New York • San Francisco • Cleveland • New Haven, Conn. • Waterville, Maine • London • Munich

For more information, contact
Lucent Books
27500 Drake Rd.
Farmington Hills, MI 48331-3535
Or you can visit our Internet site at http://www.gale.com

LIBRARY OF CONGRESS CATALOGING-IN-PUBLICATION DATA

Glick, Susan.
    War and Peace / by Susan Glick.
        p. cm. — (Discovering mythology)
Summary: Examines the war and peace myths of various cultures around the world, as well as the effects of these stories on everyday life.
Includes bibliographical references and index.
    ISBN 1-56006-903-1 (alk. paper)
    1. Creation—Comparative studies—Juvenile literature. 2. Mythology—Juvenile literature. 3. Folklore—Juvenile literature. [1. Creation. 2. Mythology. 3. Folklore.]
I. Title. II. Series

Contents

Foreword

Created by ancient cultures, the world's many and varied mythologies are humanity's attempt to make sense of otherwise inexplicable phenomena. Floods, drought, death, creation, evil, even the possession of knowledge—all have been explained in myth. The ancient Greeks, for example, observed the different seasons but did not understand why they changed. As a result, they reasoned that winter, a cold, dark time of year, was the result of a mother in mourning; the three months of winter were the days the goddess Demeter missed her daughter Persephone who had been tricked into spending part of her year in the underworld. Likewise, the people of India experienced recurring droughts, weeks and months during which their crops withered and their families starved. To explain the droughts, the Indians created the story of Vritra, a terrible demon who lived in the clouds and sucked up all the world's moisture. And the Vikings, in their search for an understanding of wisdom and knowledge, created Odin, their culture's most powerful god, who gave the world the gift of poetry and possessed two mythic ravens named Thought and Memory.

The idea of myth, fantastic stories that answer some of humanity's most enduring questions, spans time, distance, and differing cultural ideologies. Humans—whether living in the jungles of South America, along the rocky coasts of northern Europe, or on the islands of Japan—all formulated stories in an attempt to understand their world. And although their worlds differed greatly, they sometimes found similar ways of explaining the unknown or unexplainable events of their lives. Other times, there were differences, but the method of explanation—the myth—remains the same.

Each book in the Discovering Mythology series revolves around a specific topic—for example, death and the underworld; monsters; or heroes—and each chapter examines a selection of myths related to that topic. This allows young readers to note both the similarities and differences across cultures and time. Almost all cultures have myths to explain creation and death, for instance, but the actual stories sometimes vary widely. The Babylonians believed that the earth was the offspring of primordial parents, while the Navajo Indians of North America assert that the world emerged over time much like an infant grows into an adult. In ancient Greek mythology, a deceased person passed quickly into the underworld, a physical place that offered neither reward nor punishment for one's deeds in life. Egyptian myths, on the other hand, contended that a person's quality of existence in the afterlife, an ambiguous state of being, depended on his actions on earth.

In other cases, the symbolic creature or hero and what it represents are the same, but the purpose of the story may be different. Although monster myths in different cultures may not always explain the same phenomenon or offer insight into the same ethical quandary, monsters nearly always represent evil. The shape-shifting beastmen of ancient Africa represented the evils of trickery and wile. These vicious animal-like creatures transformed themselves into attractive, charming humans to entrap unsuspecting locals. Persia's White Demon devoured townspeople and nobles alike; it took the intelligence and strength of an extraordinary prince to defeat the monster and save the countryside. Even the Greek Furies, although committing their evil acts in the name of justice, were ugly, violent creatures who murdered people guilty of killing others. Only the goddess Athena could tame them.

The Discovering Mythology series presents the myths of many cultures in a format accessible to young readers. Fully documented secondary source quotes and numerous mythological tales enliven the text. Sidebars highlight interesting stories, creatures, and traditions. Annotated bibliographies offer ideas for further research. Each book in this engaging series provides students with a wealth of information as well as launching points for further discussion.

Mythical Worlds of Conflict and Peace

War plays a role in the oldest stories on earth, including the mythical tales of battling gods and monsters, or heroes engaged in combat on the battlefield. War stories, sometimes in gruesome detail, are entertaining, as modern audiences know. However, myths of war serve other purposes as well. They may provide a culture with a way to express fears. They may be a way to motivate an army or inspire loyalty. Still another purpose for myths of war might be to define and illustrate a culture's values.

Charles Freeman, in *The Greek Achievement,* understands this when he explains the significance of Homer's great epics: "In fifth-century Athens boys would learn the poems by heart and not only absorb a heritage but understand the appropriate behavior for people in different stations in life, men and women, slave and free, ruler and ruled. There was virtually no situation, either in the ways

humans relate to each other or to the way the gods relate to men and the natural world, that is not covered somewhere in the epics."[1]

What is courage? What does it mean to grieve? What good is served by fighting? What does a peaceful world look like? Myths answer these questions.

Mythical warriors, like their human counterparts, engage in war for a reason. Commonly, fighting may be to restore order. This occurs in creation myths when, almost universally, life begins in chaos and order is restored through a battle between the early gods, such as the one between the frost giants and the gods of the cold north. Mythical warriors also fight to gain territory or to retrieve something taken from them, as did the Tuatha Dé Danann when they defended their homeland, Ireland. Sometimes mythical warriors fight for honor and for the love of their country, as did Homer's heroes on the

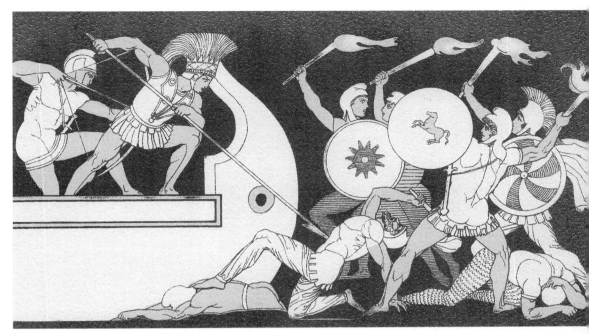

This illustration depicts the mythical Greek warrior Ajax defending his ship from Trojan soldiers. Stories of conflict and the feats of great warriors are among the world's oldest myths.

battlefield at Troy. Finally, warriors may fight because fate has determined that it must be so, as did Arjuna in India's great epic *Mahabharata* when Krishna told him that to be a warrior was his destined duty.

All cultures, too, engage in war with a clear concept of peace. Peace, or an end to the fighting, is never far from the thoughts of the warrior, even in myth. That is why even Achilles, a relentless soldier on the battlefield, carried a tranquil scene of home on the front of his shield. The Hindus knew peace as that ultimate reality, Brahman. The Norse and Celts envisioned peace as a place where food and drink were plentiful and fights could be fought without harm to the participants. For the Maya, peace was a light-filled world where the seasons followed an orderly pattern. No matter what form an enemy might take—a fierce wolf, a ten-headed demon, the deadly Bull of Heaven—the impulse to confront it, destroy it, and return to a life without conflict seems to be universal.

Ancient Battles Between the Babylonian Gods of Creation

Mesopotamia, the region now occupied by Iraq, produced some of the oldest myths in the world, dating back over five thousand years. In the fertile farmland between the Euphrates and Tigris Rivers, a rich civilization flourished. But this was also a region of much turbulence. For the ancient settlers in this floodplain, the forces of chaos were as close as the unpredictable rivers that dominated this region. Fed by melting snow off the mountains, the rivers could rise violently in the spring. Mesopotamians were adept at channeling the seasonal torrents, but the waters were still capable of much destruction. Adding to this destruction were other challenging features of a desert climate: months of devastating drought,

desert heat, dust storms, locust invasions, and hot winds, or simooms.

Despite these conditions, the people of this region prospered. The land along the rivers was not only fertile for farming, but the silt from the flooding rivers also produced a clay that was used to build the early cities for which this ancient civilization is known. The rivers, too, were a highway for trading, with caravans carrying products overland to be shipped by water throughout the Persian Gulf. This contact with the larger world brought wealth, but it also brought conflict as invading people fought for control of this valuable land.

A Series of Invaders

The Sumerians were conquered by the Akkadians, who invaded in 2300 B.C. and established Babylonia as their center. The Akkadians, also called Babylonians, were eventually conquered by the Assyrians from northern Mesopotamia. But this group fell, too, when the Persians conquered the Assyrians in 539 B.C. For thousands of years, this region saw strife from outside invaders. In addition, the people of Mesopotamia fought among themselves as city-states battled for dominance.

The mythology of this region reflects both the turbulent forces of nature and the experience of war by the peoples who lived there in city-states. The earliest gods of Mesopotamia represented the forces of nature and included sky and storm deities. The people loved these gods and built temples to individual gods. Each city had its own patron god who, it was believed, was there to protect its people. Each city also had an earthly king, said to be chosen by the patron deity. In the earliest days of Sumer (the city-states located in what

is now southern Iraq), mythical tales were part of an oral tradition, but later these stories were written on clay tablets that are still being discovered, long buried in the libraries of temples.

Early Battles in the *Epic of Creation*

One of these discoveries was the *Epic of Creation*, or the *Enuma Elish*. The *Epic of Creation*, like many creation myths around the world, began with a battle between the gods before the world of humans existed. In its simplest form, it is a battle between the forces of chaos and the forces of order. In this myth, the gods were Tiamat and Apsu, both gods of water. Apsu was the male god of fresh- or sweet water, while Tiamat was the female god of saltwater from the ocean.

Tiamat gave birth to a son who would become an important figure in Mesopotamian myth. He was called Anu and was

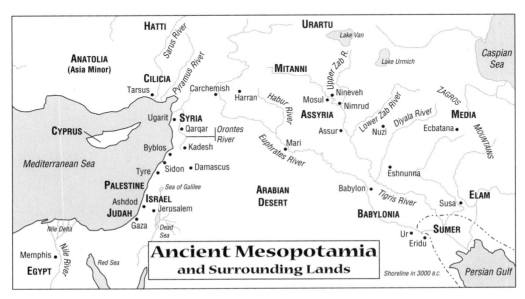

Ancient Mesopotamia
and Surrounding Lands

god of the sky. Anu's own son, Ea, would also become a powerful figure as god of the underground waters. Ea would, in time, become a ruler of all gods, even surpassing his father.

With these figures in place, the fight between the older and younger gods began. The source of conflict, oddly enough, was noise. The younger gods, Anu, Ea, and the others, were disturbing the peace of the old god Apsu. Apsu complained to Tiamat, his wife. Stephanie Dalley translates this passage in *Myths from Mesopotamia*: "Their ways have become very grievous to me, / By day I cannot rest, by night I cannot sleep. / I shall abolish their ways and dis-perse them! / Let peace prevail, so that we can sleep."[2] After repeated requests to curb the noise, Apsu had had enough. He threatened to destroy the younger gods. Tiamat protested, but Apsu was determined to kill his offspring.

When news of Apsu's intentions reached the younger gods, Ea, god of underground waters, took charge. Thinking he had the solution that would restore peace, Ea used a magic spell to make his great-grandfather sleep and then killed him. With Apsu dead, Ea was free to take the god's crown and put it on his own head. Pleased with his new-found power, Ea returned home to his wife, who soon bore a son, the storm god Marduk.

Tiamat's Fearless Demons

In the ancient myths of Mesopotamia, passages are often repeated over and over again, dramatically heightening the tension of the scene. Here, from *Myths from Mesopotamia*, is Stephanie Dalley's translation of the oft-repeated passage that describes Tiamat's demonic crew, created for her by Mother Hubur, a primordial mother goddess.

Mother Hubur, who fashions all things,
Contributed an unfaceable weapon: she bore giant snakes,
Sharp of tooth and unsparing of fang (?).
She filled their bodies with venom instead of blood.
She cloaked ferocious dragons with fearsome rays,
And made them bear mantles of radiance, made them godlike,
(chanting this imprecation)
"Whoever looks upon them shall collapse in utter terror!
Their bodies shall rear up continually, and never turn away!"
She stationed a horned serpent, a mušhuššu-dragon, and a lahmu-hero,
Ugallu-demons, a rabid dogs, and a scorpion-man,
Aggressive úmu-demons, a fish-man, and a bull-man
Bearing merciless weapons, fearless in battle.

The Powerful Marduk

Marduk, son of Ea, was outstanding from the start and far superior to his own father. Marduk, favored grandson of Anu, was given the four winds and made the god of storm. But a storm god is often a god of unrest. And such was the case with Marduk. His winds and storms disturbed Tiamat and the other gods. The gods around Tiamat rose up together, convincing her that the younger gods had already killed her husband, Apsu, and now they were disturbing them further with their whirlwinds and dust storms. It was time to retaliate. It was time for war.

The fearsome goddess Tiamat, commonly portrayed as a dragon, a creature associated with water, gathered together her forces and declared war against Ea and all who had aided him. Tamra Andrews offers this description of her in *Dictionary of Nature Myths*: "Tiamat had the body of a python, the jaws of a crocodile, the teeth of a lion, the wings of a bat, the legs of a lizard, the talons of an eagle, and the horns of a bull. She was fearsome and monstrous, and engaging her in combat was no small task."[3] She assembled a band of monsters to battle at her side, including dragons, demons, a rabid dog, a scorpion man—and a serpent filled with venom, not blood. Tiamat was so powerful, so commanding, that no one could defy her. Then she brought forward the warrior Kingu as the leader of her band of ferocious beasts, attaching to Kingu's chest a magical tool, the Tablet of Destinies. The Tablet of Destinies, notes John Gray in *Near Eastern Mythology*, was a "divine blue-print, like

The Babylonian storm god Marduk established himself as the most powerful god in the Babylonian pantheon.

the 'word of God' in Israel,"[4] giving the commander in chief Kingu instructions to carry out.

Marduk Faces Tiamat

With the powerful Tiamat preparing for battle, Ea began to fear the outcome. He sent his father to talk to Tiamat, but the goddess of saltwaters would not be calmed. She was ready to fight. Ea and his forces needed to find a powerful weapon of their own. That weapon, it was decided, would

The Lure of the Battlefield

In the myth *Erra and Ishum*, translated by Stephanie Dalley in *Myths from Mesopotamia*, Erra, the war god, has gotten so lazy that his own weapons call to him, encouraging him to return to the battlefield.

They said to Erra, "Rise! Stand up!
Why do you stay in town like a feeble old man?
How can you stay at home like a lisping child?
Are we to eat women's bread, like one who has never marched on to the battlefield?
Are we to be fearful and nervous as if we had no experience of war?
To go on to the battlefield is as good as a festival for young men!
Anyone who stays in town, be he a prince, will not be satisfied with bread alone;
He will be vilified in the mouths of his own people, and dishonoured.
How can he raise his hand against one who goes to the battlefield?
However great the strength of one who stays in town,
How can he prevail over one who has been on the battlefield?
City food, however fancy, cannot compare with what is cooked on the embers.
Best beer, however sweet, cannot compare with water from a water-skin.
A palace built on a platform cannot compare with the shelters of [a camp].
Go out to the battlefield, warrior Erra, make your weapons resound!"

be Marduk, son of Ea. Marduk was willing to stand up to Tiamat and her forces, but he had a price. To lead the young gods, he demanded supreme power over the universe. Dalley translates Marduk's request: "And let me, my own utterance, fix fate instead of you. / Whatever I create shall never be altered! / Let a decree from my lips never be revoked, never changed!"[5] The other gods, fearing the worst from Tiamat, agreed to his conditions.

Marduk prepared for battle. His weapons were many and powerful. God of storm, Marduk used all four winds, bolts of lightning, and flooding rains. Finally, Marduk

faced Tiamat herself. The fighting was fierce and Marduk quickly got the upper hand. Writer John Gray relates the gruesome scene when Marduk slays Tiamat:

The lord trod on the legs of
  Tiamat,
With his unsparing mace he
  crushed her skull,
When the arteries of her blood he
  had severed,
He split her like a shell-fish into
  two parts;
Half of her he set up and ceiled it
  as sky,

Pulled down the bar and posted
guards.

He bade them to allow not her
waters to escape.

He quartered the heavens and sur-
veyed the regions. . . .

He constructed stations for the
great gods,

Fixing their astral likenesses as
constellations.

He determined the year by designating the zones:

He set up three constellations for
each of the twelve months. . . .

The Moon he caused to shine, the
night to him entrusting,

He appointed him a creature of
the night to signify the days.[6]

With the stars in the heavens, the sun
and moon designating the rhythm of the
days, and the constellations signaling the
seasons, Marduk's creation was almost
complete. Only the body of Kingu, leader
of Tiamat's forces, remained. Marduk
seized the Tablet of Destinies for himself
and took the blood of Kingu and from it
formed the human race, suggesting, states
John Gray, "a recognition perhaps of the
daemonic, rebellious element in human
nature."[7]

Peace Restored

Following all this work, the gods rejoiced.
They gathered together for a banquet that
signaled a new beginning. In merriment,
they filled their plates with food, their
glasses with drink, and rejoiced in song and
conversation. This celebration of peace
ended with the declaration of Marduk as
the highest god, the king of all heaven and
earth.

The banquet became an important part
of the yearly New Year ritual when the
entire *Epic of Creation* was read aloud and
Marduk was honored with ceremonies and
rituals. In Marduk's city, Babylon, where
a ziggurat (a pyramid-shaped tower) was
built in his honor, the yearly ritual included an elaborate parade or procession.
During the procession, the statue of
Marduk was placed in a chariot (a two-
wheeled cart) of precious gold and stones
and led by the king through the streets.
Afterward, a banquet was held in Marduk's
honor, re-creating the banquet of the gods.

Patron Gods and Earthly Kings

With Marduk as its patron god, Babylon
felt entitled to supremacy over other
cities. Writes Stephen Bertman in his
Handbook to Life in Ancient Mesopotamia,
"In the politics of earth, the ascendancy
of Babylon's patron god Marduk as ruler
of the universe symbolized and theologi-
cally justified Babylon's own ascendancy
over the other cities of Mesopotamia and
their local gods."[8] But other cities relied
on their protector gods as well. The earthly king relied on the power of their mythical god or goddess, calling on the deity
for success both on the battlefield against
foreign invaders and during conflicts with
armies from neighboring cities.

The city-states of early Mesopotamia
were surrounded by thick, high walls to

protect them against attack. The early soldiers drew on an extensive array of weaponry. They used spears, bows, arrows, and shields. Chariots were an early invention by the Sumerians. Cavalry, fighters on horseback, followed later. Archaeologists have unearthed artwork that was commissioned by the victorious king. These clay slabs or seals depict the scenes of war and many details about fighting methods and weaponry. Some of the artwork includes mythical battles between the gods of order and chaos, for example.

Gilgamesh Fights for Fame

Another figure found on the cylinder seals is that of Gilgamesh, one of the oldest of the world's mythical heroes. His story is told in the epic of Gilgamesh. Gilgamesh, a figure based on an actual king of the Babylonian city Uruk, was willing to fight whatever forces stood in the way of his achieving immortality and fame. Gilgamesh was no ordinary man, but was blessed by the gods with superior traits. According to the N.K. Sandars translation of *The Epic*

The Babylonians honored Marduk with a massive pyramid-shaped temple known as a ziggurat in the very heart of the city.

of *Gilgamesh*, "When the gods created Gilgamesh they gave him a perfect body. Shamash the glorious sun endowed him with beauty, Adad the god of the storm endowed him with courage, the great gods made his beauty perfect, surpassing all others, terrifying like a great wild bull. Two thirds they made him god and one third man."[9]

When Gilgamesh left Uruk and set out to achieve fame, the gods provided him with a companion and rival, a shaggy-haired mountain man and warrior named Enkidu. Enkidu, too, was strong, a worthy match for the near-perfect Gilgamesh. The two were pitted against each other in a wrestling match in the public square. Their fighting was so violent that the door frames and walls of nearby buildings shook. The confrontation did not last long before the two decided that rather than fight, they would be better suited as partners. Enkidu suggested they join together and journey to the Pine Forest guarded by an evil giant named Humbaba, who would not let anyone enter. This battle, Gilgamesh reasoned, would earn him fame. Even if he were to be killed by the giant, Gilgamesh declared, in the Sandars translation of the epic, "men will say of me, 'Gilgamesh has fallen in fight with ferocious Humbaba.' Long after the child has been born in my house, they will say it, and remember."[10]

Confronting Humbaba

Before the two friends faced the giant, they called on Shamash to help them, promising to build a temple to the god in return. Shamash was persuaded. So when

In The Epic of Gilgamesh, *Enkidu and Gilgamesh defeat the evil demon Humbaba (shown) by cutting off his head.*

Gilgamesh was in the midst of his fight with the giant, he cried out to Shamash. Writes Sandars,

> Glorious Shamash heard his prayer and he summoned the great wind, the north wind, the whirlwind, the storm and the icy wind, the tempest and the scorching wind; they came like dragons, like a scorching fire, like a serpent that freezes the heart, a destroying flood and the lightning's fork. The eight winds rose up against Humbaba, they beat against his eyes; he was gripped, unable to go forward or back.[11]

Humbaba begged Enkidu for mercy, but Enkidu refused. Encouraged by Enkidu, Gilgamesh cut off the giant's head and the two friends exalted in their victory.

Gilgamesh Tangles with Ishtar and the Bull of Heaven

After this fight, Gilgamesh was rewarded by the admiration of the earth-mother goddess Ishtar, who offered him marriage and a chariot of precious jewels, lapis lazuli (a clear blue semiprecious stone), gold, and all kinds of riches. But Gilgamesh knew all about the insatiable Ishtar and her mistreatment of her lovers. He decided to confront her, recounting in detail the harm she had brought to those who dared to care about her, including the time she broke her bird-lover's wing, the gardener she turned into a frog, and the poor shepherd who cooked lamb for her every day but was rewarded by being transformed into a wolf for his own dogs to tear apart.

Ishtar was disgraced and angered by Gilgamesh's words and went to her father, Anu, and begged him to create the monstrous Bull of Heaven and pit it against Gilgamesh. Anu was reluctant to do so because unleashing the Bull of Heaven against Uruk meant seven years of drought for the city. But when Ishtar threatened to break the doors of hell and bring back the dead to earth, Anu agreed. The Bull of Heaven was a fearsome beast who could open a chasm in the earth's surface by merely snorting. With each snort, hundreds of men fell into the chasm

and met their deaths. Against the bull, Enkidu, too, stumbled, but was able to return to his feet.

Gilgamesh rushed to his friend's aid, stabbing the bull in the throat, plunging his sword into the bull's head, between his horns, and then pulling out the bull's insides. The Bull of Heaven was dead, and Gilgamesh and Enkidu, proud warriors, returned to their city to brag of their endeavors and to enjoy the fame that the city bestowed on them. For a short while, they triumphed in their victory, feasting and celebrating. The women of the town called to Gilgamesh. Translates Sandars, "Gilgamesh is the most glorious of heroes, Gilgamesh is the most eminent among men."[12] However, this joy would not last. Enkidu dreamed that night that he was destined to die. In his dream the gods informed him that he had insulted Ishtar when he refused to grant mercy to the giant Humbaba. When Enkidu awoke, he knew the dream would come true, for he was stricken and suffering and unable to rise from his bed.

Death of the Warrior Enkidu

Enkidu had no wish to die and railed at the sun god Shamash. He had had a glimpse of afterlife in his dream and it was a dreary, dim place. He was not ready to go there. Shamash responded, telling Enkidu that his death was inevitable but not to be ungrateful for all that she had given him. She reminded him that he would be mourned and lamented over when he was gone. While versions differ, in the Sandars

Ishtar, Mother Warrior

Ishtar was one of those goddesses who was both a mother goddess and a deity of war. She was the goddess of the life-giving forces of motherhood, vegetation, and love, but she also appeared on the battlefield in warrior garb. She was said to be associated with Venus, the star that appeared in the morning with the sun and lit the skies at night. The myths that feature her sometimes present a confusing array of characteristics. Even her position among the gods is not clear. She is said to be the sister of sun god Shamash. But she is also the daughter of sky god Anu.

One of her most famous encounters in the land of myth is her descent into the underworld, where she lied to the gatekeeper Neti, telling him that she was the sister of Ereshkigal, queen of the under-

world. To reach Ereshkigal, Ishtar had to go through seven gates, following a ritual of being stripped of a piece of clothing or jewelry at each gate, beginning with the crown on her head. Finally, quite naked, Ishtar reached Ereshkigal, who knew, of course, that this intruder was not her sister. Ereshkigal killed the goddess and hung up her corpse. Ishtar did not stay dead for long, though. She was rescued by her companion, Ninshubar, who solicited help from the other gods, who restored Ishtar to life.

Ishtar (center) was both a mother goddess and a deity of war.

translation, Enkidu could not be com-
forted and died bitter that he did not fall
on the battlefield and die a warrior's honorable death. In other versions, he calm-
ly accepts his fate.

*Despite his long quest for eternal life,
Gilgamesh (pictured) accepts his mortality
at the conclusion of the tale.*

At the passing of his friend, Gilgamesh
went into a deep mourning, deeply lament-
ing the loss of his friend, just as Shamash
had promised. In this state, Gilgamesh pursued the ultimate in everlasting fame: He
wished to achieve immortality and avoid
the fate of Enkidu. He roamed the country, praying to the moon god Sin to spare
him death.

Utnapishtim Advises Gilgamesh

In his quest for immortality, Gilgamesh
faced several more obstacles, such as the
Scorpion-Man, who guarded the mountains at the edge of the world. He also met
an alehouse keeper who encouraged him
to stop his roaming and grieving and to
enjoy his life, to make each day a day of
feasting, to let his stomach fill with wine
and food, to wash his hair and clothes, and
to take delight in children and a spouse.

But Gilgamesh would have none of this,
so the alehouse keeper gave up and directed him to the boatman Utnapishtim, who
had the power to ferry Gilgamesh over the
waters into the land of death. Gilgamesh
demanded eternal life but Utnapishtim
refused him. Instead, Utnapishtim told him
the story of how he, himself, had obtained
it by being the one who survived an ancient
flood. After hearing this, Gilgamesh continued to beg for eternal life. Even though
Utnapishtim set up a trial test for Gilgamesh, asking him to stay awake six days and
seven nights, the tired demigod could not
achieve it.

In one final challenge, Gilgamesh was
given the opportunity to find and hold the

magical plant that would grant immortality. But when Gilgamesh came upon it at the bottom of a pool, a serpent snatched it away. Gilgamesh wept with disappointment. The epic of Gilgamesh concludes with his recognizing and accepting the fact he is mortal, and no battle on earth will win eternal life for him.

Ninurta Defeats the Evil Anzu

The myth of Gilgamesh was popular; it has been uncovered in many sites throughout the Middle East. Other shorter myths also dealt with significant battles for control and power. One such occurred between Ninurta, the god of war, and Anzu, the evil son of sky god Anu. Ninurta appears later in the myth, which begins with the troublemaker Anzu, acting as a servant to the earth god Enlil. Anzu, a god in the form of a bird, was hungry for power. He saw the Tablet of Destinies, the same one held by Kingu in the war against Marduk, in Enlil's hands and knew that whoever held the Tablet of Destinies would be the master of all the gods. It was not long before Anzu boldly stole the tablet while Enlil was bathing and flew off with it, sending Enlil and the other gods into a panic. Sky god Anu began calling for a god who would face Anzu and fight for the return of the tablet. Dalley translates the fearful reply that was repeated by each of the gods:

Father, who could rush off to the
    inaccessible mountain?

Which of the gods your sons will
    be Anzu's conqueror?

For he has gained the Tablet of
    Destinies for himself,

Has taken away the [Enlil]-power:
    rites are abandoned!

Anzu flew off and went into hiding!

His utterance has replaced that of
    Duranki's god;

He has only to command, and
    whoever he curses turns to clay!

At his utterance the gods (must
    now) tremble! [13]

When each of the gods repeated these exact words, the gods began to despair of ever finding someone brave enough and powerful enough to win back the tablet. Finally, Ea had a brainstorm. He decided that Belet-ili, one of his sisters, could create a new god, a powerful god who could take on Anzu, kill him, and return the tablet. Belet-ili did so. She created Ninurta and then called to the other gods to lend him aid.

With the power of seven evil winds behind him, Ninurta went forth. He was armed with a powerful bow. The battle against Anzu was not an easy one. Ninurta aimed his arrow at the evil Anzu, but each time, the shaft turned and the arrow came back. "Deadly silence came over the battle," Dalley relates, "and conflict ceased. Weapons stopped, and did not capture Anzu amid the mountains." [14] But Ninurta did not give up. Finally, he was able to kill Anzu and return with the tablet. Enlil and the gods were pleased. Dagan, god of the underworld, called out, "Let him come to us, / Let him rejoice, play, make merry."[15] And Ninurta was honored for his brave deeds, and all the gods called out his name.

The Mesopotamians lived in a world where the elements of nature wielded much power. The destructive forces of floods, droughts, winds, and rains came to be reflected in their myths. The fighting between deities, or between the deities and the mortals who opposed them, sometimes brought order. But more often the battles of myth reflected the continual conflicts of a people frequently at war either with the natural world or with power-seeking invaders who kept them from experiencing the peace they desired.

Power Struggles in the Aegean

Chapter Two

The tales of the argumentative and interfering Greek gods, told long before Homer or anyone else recorded them, reflect a culture that knew both the upheaval and disruption of war, and the peaceful life of farming or fishing in the sunny climate of the Aegean. The Greek culture had its roots in the island of Crete, a peaceful agrarian civilization that began five thousand years ago. For many years, this culture, called Minoan, dominated the region, but eventually, about 1450 B.C., the more aggressive and warlike Mycenaeans, who had moved in from the north and settled on the mainland of Greece, conquered Minoan Crete.

The skirmishes continued, however, with the growth of the polis, or city-state, as the Mycenaeans built fortified cities, with kings who lived in palaces and fought for domination. In fact, writes Bernard Knox in his introduction to Robert Fagles' *Homer: The Iliad*, the Greeks "were almost uninterruptedly at war with one another." Knox continues, "The Greek29 *polis*, the city-state, was a communi-

ty surrounded by potential enemies, who could turn into actual belligerents at the first sign of aggression or weakness."[16] Athens, with its navy fleet, and Sparta, with its trained army, provide an example of two powerful city-states with a strong rivalry between them, although they did unite against foreign invaders.

All the while that war was upon them, the Greeks strove to live a peaceful life as farmers. They raised sheep and goats and planted crops such as olives and grapes, which took years to cultivate. As much as the Greeks loved stories of war, in actuality war took men from their homes and left women and children, sometimes with the aid of slaves, to struggle on their own, farming on hilly terrain in arid, rocky soil.

Early Power Struggles in the Time of the Titans

The early creation myths of the Greeks may very well reflect both this clashing of cultures between the Mycenaeans and the Minoans and the struggles of farmers

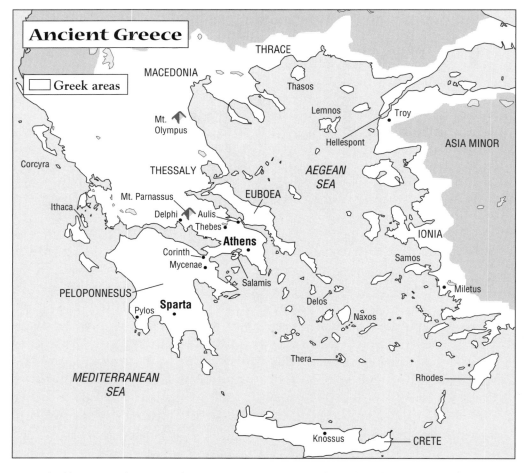

Ancient Greece

☐ Greek areas

THRACE
MACEDONIA
Thasos
Lemnos
Troy
Mt. Olympus
Hellespont
ASIA MINOR
Corcyra
THESSALY
AEGEAN SEA
Mt. Parnassus
EUBOEA
Ithaca
Delphi
Aulis
Thebes
IONIA
Athens
Corinth
Samos
Mycenae
Miletus
Salamis
PELOPONNESUS
Delos
Sparta
Naxos
Pylos
Thera
MEDITERRANEAN SEA
Rhodes
Knossus
CRETE

in a challenging climate. The creation myths tell of a universe that in its earliest stages was dominated by conflicts. In *Theogony*, Hesiod describes the beginning as a state where only a dark vastness called Chaos existed. Then there appeared Gaea, mother earth, and Eros, the force of love. Other elements followed, such as night and day, and the waters of the earth. Gaea, mother earth, gave birth to Uranus, who was the sky above and her equal.

It was when Gaea and Uranus had children together that the conflicts began, as Uranus hated each of his children. The first offspring of Gaea and Uranus were a race called the Titans. Then they produced a one-eyed monster called Cyclops, followed by three terrible monsters. Uranus took all of his children and hid them in a cave, deep in the earth.

Gaea, their mother, was horrified at what Uranus had done. Gaea asked Cronus, one of her children, to help her seek revenge against Uranus. Gaea created a curved blade, a sickle, and gave it to Cronus as a weapon. Together, mother and son waited for Uranus to come to Gaea at night and then Cronus struck his father, castrating him and casting his private parts to the ground where his blood seeped deep into the earth. This blood produced more monsters in the form of Giants, a race called the Furies, and ash nymphs.

The conflict with Uranus was over, but his son Cronus would create troubles of his own. First, however, Cronus freed his siblings and continued with the work of creating the world. Such features of the world as the rivers, the moon, the sun, and much more came into being. After this was done, Cronus took his sister Rhea as his wife. Cronus, like his father before him, did not want his children to live, so, as each was born, Cronus swallowed the child. Hestia, Demeter, Hera, Hades, and Poseidon all met this fate.

Zeus, the last to be born, was spared. Rhea could not bear to see one more

Peaceful Places

The ancient Greeks envisioned other worlds beyond their own where people lived in peace and bliss. To the north and east, back behind the north winds and on the other side of a mountain range, were the happy lands of the Hyperboreans. The Isles of the Blessed lay to the west. Anyone who had pleased the gods could end up there. To the south of the seas was a place of no war. This was home for the lucky Ethiopians.

child be destroyed, so she tricked her husband, giving him a stone wrapped in baby blankets, and hid the real baby, Zeus, in the forest on the island of Crete. When Cronus eventually came looking for him, the Curetes, a tribe of warrior priests, protected him from being discovered. Zeus grew up with nymphs and goats, living a peaceful existence in the forest. When he became a man, he returned to his father and with the help of Metis, the daughter of Oceanus, gave him a drink that made him throw up the children he had swallowed. And Zeus, with his brothers and sisters, went to reside on Mount Olympus.

War with the Titans

However, a problem remained. The Titans, that earlier race that was the offspring of Gaea and Uranus, were not about to relinquish control to the gods of Olympus. War raged for ten years. Eager to end the conflict once and for all, Zeus descended to the underworld where the monsters borne by Uranus and Gaea were being kept prisoners. Zeus brought them out of the dark underworld and into the light and appealed to them for help. M.L. West translates this passage from Hesiod's *Theogony*:

> Hearken to me, proud children of Earth and Heaven [Gaea and Uranus], and let me say what the spirit in my breast bids me. For long now we have been fighting each other for victory and power, day after day, the Titan gods and we who were born of

[Cronus]. But now you must display great strength and your terrible hands against the Titans in the fearful slaughter, remembering our faithful friendship, and how much you suffered before our decision brought you back into the light from your dismal bondage down in the misty darkness. [17]

The monsters, Campe, the Hecatoncheires, and Cyclops, were inspired to fight for Zeus and the other gods of Olympus. They grew for themselves a hundred more

A bronze head of Zeus, the supreme Greek god who overthrew the old gods, the Titans, and took control of Mount Olympus.

arms and fifty more heads and then went forth into battle, determined to slaughter. Both sides fought hard. The earth and sky shook with their battle sounds. Zeus joined them, unleashing his full strength, casting lightning flashes and thunderbolts, until the forests and earth burned.

Zeus's allies, the monsters, seeing their leader thus engaged, stepped up their own fighting, putting rocks into their many, many hands, until the sky was blackened with rock-missiles. Not long after, the war ended, with Zeus and his siblings assuming the power of Mount Olympus. The Titans were bound and thrown into the depths of the earth.

Mother Earth Fights Back

Gaea did not like seeing her children, the Titans, being beaten. In revenge, she gave birth to another son, this time a serpent monster named Typhon. Typhon was a frightening opponent for Zeus. Hesiod offers this description of Typhon:

Out of his shoulders came a hundred fearsome snake-heads with black tongues flickering, and the eyes in his strange heads flashed fire under his brows; and there were voices in all his fearsome heads, giving out every kind of indescribable sound. Sometimes they uttered as if for the gods' understanding, sometimes again the sound of a bellowing bull whose might is uncontainable and whose voice is proud, sometimes again of a lion who knows no re-

Zeus throws thunderbolts at the multiheaded serpent, Typhon. Zeus scorched every one of Typhon's heads until the beast fell dead.

straint, sometimes again of a pack of hounds, astonishing to hear; sometimes again he hissed; and the long mountains echoed beneath.[18]

Typhon created winds and fire and earthquakes.

Zeus struck back. He used his thunderbolts and scorched every head of the monster until the monster fell wounded to the ground. With his defeat, Typhon melted the earth beneath him. Typhon also left behind the strong winds that sweep the earth, especially those bitter and forceful winds that sink ships at sea.

Battle Against the Giants

In some versions of the early myths, the gods on Olympus had scarcely settled themselves when new fighting ensued. This time the battle was against the

Giants, those monsters who had been created from the blood of Uranus as it seeped down into the earth. Leading the attack against Mount Olympus were the giants Porphyrion and Alcyoneus. Like the other creatures, these two beasts had legs of snakes and feet formed like the heads of reptiles.

The landforms around Olympus sank beneath the fierce attack of the Giants. Mountains, islands, and rivers all disappeared in their wake. The Giants used their bodies, piled one upon the other, to scale the walls of Mount Olympus. The gods retaliated against this formidable force, using swords and spears to slay the invaders. But the two leaders, Alcyoneus and Porphyrion, were not so easily killed. The gods had decreed that Alcyoneus would only die by a mortal's hands and away from his homeland, so it took half-mortal Heracles to kill him, but only after he transported him to the foreign land of Pallene. Porphyrion was also killed by the intervention of the gods. Zeus cast a spell on him in which the giant would fall in love with Hera, Zeus's wife and queen of Mount Olympus. In doing so, Porphyrion was left vulnerable and, again, Heracles was able to shoot him with a deadly arrow.

The defeat of the monsters explained for the Greeks some of the physical landscape of their world. The skin of one of the slain Giants formed the sea; another was buried under the island of Sicily. When he rolled over, the island shook with the motion of an earthquake.

Harmony on Mount Olympus

When the gods were not facing attacks from giants, or fighting among themselves, Mount Olympus could be a peaceful place for the twelve main gods and goddesses and the numerous minor gods who gathered there. Zeus ruled over the gods with a watchful eye and a stern insistence on order. He insisted that gods who did not obey him would be punished appropriately. Zeus could be harsh and mete out severe punishments with his thunderbolts, but he was also a protective god who enforced just and fair laws. It can be said that Zeus provided a good model of leadership and kingly behavior.

Zeus's Mount Olympus was a comfortable haven for the gods. It was portrayed as a serene place where food and drink were plentiful. Notes Félix Guirand in *Greek Mythology,* "Seated around their golden tables the gods dined on celestial nectar and ambrosia, and savoured the rising fragrance of fatted cattle which mortals burned in their honour on their altars below."[19] The air was filled with the sounds of Apollo's harp and the singing of the Muses. And the gods enjoyed the special privilege of eternal youth: No matter what wounds were inflicted upon them by mortals or monsters, the gods were able to heal and resume their previous forms.

Revolt Against Zeus

Despite the generally peaceful atmosphere on Mount Olympus, the gods occasionally engaged in conflicts over power. One example of a serious fight between the gods occurred between Zeus and his wife, Hera. Zeus was an unfaithful husband. In many myths, he was involved with other goddesses, nymphs, and mortal women. Hera was not pleased and nagged her husband constantly about his infidelity. She even retaliated against the women Zeus had been involved with, punishing them for their role in it, no matter how hapless.

Finally, Hera had had enough. She solicited the aid of Poseidon and Apollo and launched a plan to keep Zeus from leaving Olympus. While he slept, Hera, Poseidon, and Apollo worked together and bound Zeus with leather so that he could not move either his arms or his legs. When Zeus awoke, his first wish was to kill all three of them. But Zeus's arms were tied and he could not grab the thunderbolt, his weapon of choice. Hera and the others left Zeus tied and bound and gathered with the other gods of Olympus to decide who would take over as chief of the gods.

Many of the gods and goddesses wanted to take over the role that Zeus had held. The deities argued among themselves for a long time, their jealousy and anger toward one another mounting. They were no better off than when Zeus had been in charge. Writes Ellen Switzer in *Greek Myths: Gods, Heroes, and Monsters,* "While they were quarreling, Nereid, a female Titan who had been spared when Zeus banished all the Titan males, decided that anything would be better than another civil war on Olympus, even Zeus with all his faults. So she untied the knots and released Zeus to wreak vengeance on his disobedient relatives."[20] Once Zeus was free, punishment was swift. Apollo and Poseidon were sent to live on earth as servants until some time had passed, and they promised never again to disobey. Hera's punishment was even worse. She was suspended from the sky by her bound wrists, her ankles weighted down with heavy anvils. She, too, was

Ares: Unpopular God of War

Ares, the son of Zeus and Hera, was the most hated of the gods on Olympus. He was argumentative, brutal, and impulsive. His own family did not like him. He fought with his sister, Athena, and even his parents did not respect him. During the Trojan War when Ares is wounded on the battlefield, his father, Zeus, refuses him sympathy for his wounds, accusing him of interfering too much in the war. In Homer's *Iliad*, translated by Richmond Lattimore, Zeus tells Ares just what he thinks of him.

Do not sit beside me and whine, you double-faced liar.
To me you are the most hateful of all the gods who hold Olympos.
Forever quarrelling is dear to your heart, wars and battles.

eventually freed, but only after Zeus was convinced she would not revolt against him again.

The Two Sides of Athena

Despite Hera's displeasure with Zeus, the king of the gods did not stop in his pursuit of other women. One such dalliance resulted in the birth of the goddess Athena. Athena had an interesting birth. Her mother was the sea nymph Metis, daughter of the sea god. When Zeus heard that he would die by the hand of his own son, he impulsively swallowed Metis and her unborn child. The result of this action gave

Athena, the goddess of war, wisdom, and a patron of arts and crafts, sprang from the head of Zeus after the blacksmith Hephaestus split the god's head with an ax to cure his headache.

Zeus a tremendous headache, and he begged the blacksmith Hephaestus to help him. Hephaestus split open Zeus's head with an ax and out of it emerged a full-grown goddess, dressed in full body armor.

Athena would become Zeus's favorite child. She was a frequent visitor to the battlefield, a friend to the warriors of Greek myth: Heracles, Perseus, and Achilles. Athena was often portrayed in full armor, carrying a spear and wearing a breastplate bordered with snakes. While Athena was the goddess of war, unlike her argumentative half-brother, Ares, god of war, Athena had a more gentle and peace-loving side, as well. The goddess was also associated with the crafts of peace. She was said to be the inventor of the potter's wheel and a talented weaver and spinner, and even the tamer of horses. She also assisted the Greek hero Jason with the design and building of his ship, the *Argo*. Finally, Athena's gift to the world was the olive tree, as valuable a resource then as now.

The Trojan War

The gods and goddesses of Greek myth are at the forefront of Homer's great war epic, the *Iliad*. Composed in the early eighth century B.C., the *Iliad* tells the story of the war fought between the Achaeans (or Greeks) and the Trojans over the return of Helen to her rightful husband, Menelaus. The main theme of the poem is the anger of the Greek warrior and demigod Achilles. Some historians have suggested that Homer's topic, the Trojan War, was based

on an actual event that occurred in 1200 B.C., when the Mycenaeans fought against Troy on the coast of Asia Minor, now Turkey. But it is just as likely, given the Greek love of their gods and heroes, as Charles Freeman points out in *The Greek Achievement,* that the story "could be an invention, the creation of a story around a city which would be familiar to the whole Greek world, a fantasy tale of what the Mycenaeans would have liked to have achieved if they *had* been superhuman."[21]

In war, as in all other realms of Greek life, the gods of Olympus were never far away. In fact, it was the actions of the god of discord, Eris, that set in motion the events that would start the Trojan War. This triggering event took place during the wedding of King Peleus and the nymph, Thetis. During the festivities, Eris, sister of Ares, the god of war, tossed an apple into the crowd, proclaiming that the "fairest" god assembled should be the one to claim it. Hera, Athena, and Aphrodite all thought the apple should be theirs. They went to Zeus for a final decision, but he turned over that task to a young man named Paris.

Paris chose Aphrodite, who in exchange promised him the young woman, Helen. Helen, unfortunately, was already married to Menelaus, the king of Sparta, but Paris did not let that deter him. He simply kidnapped her, taking her to Troy, and the war that was fought over her return began. Agamemnon, the king of Mycenae and brother to Menelaus, led the Greeks, with such powerful warriors as Achilles, Odysseus, Nestor, Patroclos, and Ajax on his

Peace upon the Land

In *Works and Days*, Hesiod makes clear the rewards of a nonviolent life.

As for those who give straight judgments to visitors and to their own people and do not deviate from what is just, their community flourishes, and the people bloom in it. Peace is about the land, fostering the young, and wide-seeing Zeus never marks out grievous war as their portion. Neither does Famine attend straight-judging men, nor Blight, and they feast on the crops they tend. For them Earth bears plentiful food, and on the mountains the oak carries acorns at its surface and bees at its centre. The fleecy sheep are laden down with wool; the womenfolk bear children that resemble their parents; they enjoy a continual sufficiency of good things. Nor do they ply on ships, but the grain-giving ploughland bears them fruit.

But for those who occupy themselves with violence and wickedness and brutal deeds, Kronos' son, wide-seeing Zeus, marks out retribution. Often a whole community together suffers in consequence of a bad man who does wrong and contrives evil. From heaven Kronos' son brings disaster upon them, famine and with it plague, and the people waste away. The womenfolk do not give birth, and households decline, by Olympian Zeus' design. At other times again, he either destroys those men's broad army or city wall, or punishes their ships at sea.

side. The Trojans were led by King Priam, and he, too, was aided by notable fighters, such as Paris, his son, and the mighty Hector.

The gods joined these men on the battlefront, choosing sides. Aphrodite, of course, continued to aid the Trojans, as did Zeus. Hera and Athena, who did not forget Paris's choice of Aphrodite, sided with the Greeks, as did the sea god Poseidon. The actions of the gods could turn the course of the war. For example, Apollo cast a plague on the Greeks in response to their kidnapping of the daughter of a favored priest on the Trojan side. Likewise, Aphrodite rescued Paris in his decisive one-on-one battle with Menelaus that could have ended the war. Stepping directly into battle, Poseidon and Athena aided Achilles in his battle with the river god, and then, caught up in the emotion of human combat, engaged in fighting among themselves.

The Realities of the Battlefield

However, it is the actions of heroes like Achilles and Hector that illustrate most clearly the Greek attitudes toward war. Homer captures in the *Iliad* both the weariness of war that the men felt—and their duty to partake in it. Thus, when the nymph Thetis, the mother of Achilles, begged him not to fight, he told her that he would rather live a short life of glory than a long life of none. Likewise, the Trojan warrior Hector made a decision to leave his wife and young son and return to the battlefield. Observes Bernard Knox, in the introduction to Robert Fagles' translation of the *Iliad*, "She weeps and begs him to be careful, as wives have begged their husbands all through histo-ry."[22] Hector tells her that he understands her fears and desires, but he cannot avoid the battle: "All this weighs on my mind too, dear woman. / But I would die of shame to face the men of Troy / and the

Unable to dissuade her son Achilles from going into battle, Thetis brings his arms. Achilles convinced his mother that a short life of glory is better than a long life of cowardice.

Trojan women trailing their long robes / if I would shrink from battle now, a coward."[23] Even Odysseus chose to fight rather than be a coward, proclaiming:

A disgraceful thing if I should
   break and run,
fearing their main force—but it's
   far worse
if I'm taken all alone. Look, Zeus
   just drove
the rest of my comrades off in
   panic flight.
But why debate, my friend, why
   thrash things out?
Cowards, I know, would quit the
   fighting now
but the man who wants to make
   his mark in war
must stand his ground and brace
   for all he's worth—
suffer his wounds or wound his
   man to death.[24]

To live and fight with honor, to achieve excellence on the battlefield was of great importance, even though death for the Greek warrior meant a dark dismal underworld, rather than an afterlife of rewards.

Fighting with honor often meant death on the battlefield, and Homer does not spare the details of death. As Knox points out, "Men die in the *Iliad* in agony; they drop, screaming, to their knees, reaching out to beloved companions, gasping their life out, clawing the ground with their hands; they die roaring, like Asius, raging, like the great Sarpedon, bellowing, like Hippodamas, moaning, like Polydorus."[25]

The fight between Hector and Patroclos is compared, in the W.H.D. Rouse prose translation of the *Iliad,* to a fight between two animals: "And Hector leapt from his [chariot] to meet him: and there they fought as two lions fight over a deer's body, both hungry, both furious—there Patroclos Menoitiadês and glorious Hector were ready to tear each other to pieces. Hector laid hold of the head and would not let go, Patroclos held fast by the foot—and the two armies behind them were fighting too."[26] The fight continued with Patroclos killing more Trojans, until he, too, fell wounded. Hector approached to finish him off. Translates Rouse: "When Hector saw him [Patroclos] retreating and wounded, he came near and stabbed him in the belly: the blade ran through, he fell with a dull thud, and consternation took the [Greeks]. So fell Patroclos, like a wild boar killed by a lion, when both are angry and both are parched with thirst, and they fight over a little mountain pool, until the lion is too strong for the panting boar."[27]

A Hero's Anger and Grief

At the death of his dear friend, Patroclos, Achilles was so angry that he returned to war, arming himself with a new shield crafted for him by Hephaestus, god of fire. The shield was decorated with images of men fighting, but it also featured peaceful domestic scenes of children carrying baskets of fruit, dancing maidens, and sheep. Holding this shield, Achilles returned to war, fighting with a strength

Achilles (center) mourns the loss of his dear friend Patroclos, while the lifeless body of Hector lies unattended on the ground.

that was unsurpassed, even in a tale noted for its vicious fighting.

Achilles showed no mercy when he stabbed the frightened Hector in the neck. Even after Hector was dead, the anger Achilles felt was unabated. He tied Hector's feet and dragged him behind his chariot, and then, in a final cruel gesture, left his body unattended while he saw to the funeral of Patroclos.

Achilles finally returned the body when Hector's father, Priam, aided by the messenger god Iris, sneaked into the Greek camp and begged the Greek warrior to take pity. Priam pleaded with Achilles to think of how his own father must feel, to consider how, writes Fagles, "his old heart rejoices, hopes rising, day by day, to see his beloved son sailing home from Troy."[28]

Both men were touched by the pain of war and cried together, grieving for their own losses—Priam, over the death of Hector; Achilles, over the loss of Patroclos. Together they cursed the role of the gods in determining their lives and lamented the futility of war. Said Achilles, in the Fagles translation: "So the immortals spun our lives that we, we wretched men / live on to bear such torments—the gods live free of sorrows."[29]

In the end, Achilles, as fated, died, too, when pierced in the ankle by an arrow of Paris. The Greeks, after ten years of fighting this war, finally emerged victorious. The final event, told in Homer's *Odyssey*, took place when Odysseus tricked the Trojans into bringing the enormous Trojan horse into the walls of their city so that the Greek warriors could launch a final attack.

The stories of Homer and the writing of Hesiod capture well life in early Greece—and the constant presence of the gods. Bernard Knox analyzes the function of the gods in Greek myth: They "are the personification of those mysterious forces which through their often violent interaction produce the harsh patterns of human life—the rise and fall of nations, the destructiveness of the earthquake, the ter-ror of the flood, the horrors of the plague, but also the sweetness of passionate love, the intoxication of wine, the extra strength that surges through a warrior's limbs at the moment of danger."[30]

The extended history of invasion and defense of their homeland created in the Greeks an acute awareness of all the sides of war—from the realities of the battle-field, to the grief that followed the death of loved ones, to the poignant longing of the fighting men for the families and fields they had left behind. The myths of the Greeks express all this in stories that are still meaningful today.

Warrior Magic

Chapter Three

The group of people referred to as the Celts originally lived in Europe, north of the Alps, as early as 600 B.C. For a thousand years, the Celts expanded across Europe, reaching land as far east as the modern British Isles, and as far west as Czechoslovakia and Hungary. The Celts were a warring people who lived in small villages.

The mythology of the Celts, because it spanned so much territory over so much time, is difficult to date accurately. Early Greek and Roman writers made references to the earliest of Celtic beliefs, but most of the major works of Celtic mythology were recorded after Christianity became the official religion of the Roman Empire. This late recording of a mythology that was originally an oral tradition has led scholars to debate the influence of Christian beliefs. Fortunately, along with references by classical writers, there is also some archaeological evidence that speaks to common elements in very early Celtic myth.

Many of these early myths are contained in such texts as Ireland's *The Book of In-vasions* and *The Mythical Cycle*, and the Welsh texts *Four Branches of the Mabinogi* and *Spoils of Annwn*. From these and other works, readers of modern times can gain a sense of common elements of Celtic mythology, in both the insular Ireland and Wales. Elements that characterize Celtic myth include an emphasis on the natural world, on the supernatural, and on war and the afterlife that awaited warriors.

The Celtic Warrior

The early Celts were an Iron Age people who had high regard for the warrior and the act of fighting. Like their mythical figures, the heavily armed Celts were organized into tribes led by warrior chiefs. Anne Ross, in *The Pagan Celts*, comments on the Celtic love for war: "In pagan Celtic societies . . . war was regarded as the norm, and highly desirable; and fighting and success in single combat were right and proper for the young warrior and hero-elect. The Celts were not much concerned about who fought whom or for what particular reason, or when or where the battle took place, provided some excuse could be concocted for a set-to."[31]

Information about their weaponry and dress is gained through descriptions in myth, as well as actual burial sites. Celtic warrior gear included iron swords, spears, shields, daggers, and helmets. Warriors, both mythical and real, were transported in two-wheeled war chariots from which they threw their spears. Sometimes Celtic fighters carried trumpets to confuse and frighten the enemy. All of these weapons were mentioned in the myths of warrior Cú Chulainn and other heroes.

Close single combat was a favored method of fighting. Fighting scenes were described in great detail in Celtic myth. For example, in the epic tale *The Tain*, also

called *The Cattle Raid of Cooley*, translator Thomas Kinsella offers this description of the fight between Cú Chulainn and his opponent Ferdia:

Then they fought together so closely that their heads touched at the top and their feet at the bottom and their hands in the middle around the edges and knobs of their shields. So closely they fought that their shields split and burst from rim to belly: so closely they fought that their spears bent and collapsed, worn-out from the tips to the rivets: so closely they fought that their shield-rims and sword-hilts and spear-shafts screamed like demons and devils and goblins of the glen

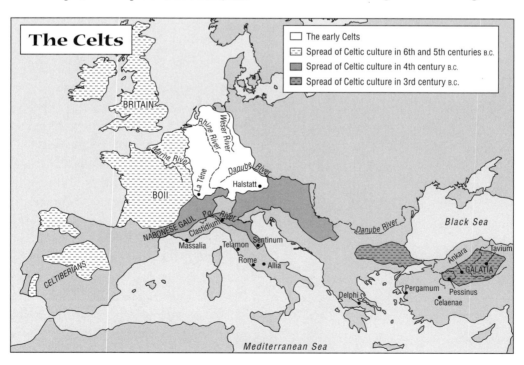

A terracotta bas-relief depicts a Celtic warrior with spoils of combat.

and fiends of the air: so closely they fought that they drove the river off its course and out of its bed. [32]

Early Mythical Warriors

The *Book of Invasions* tells the story of the occupation of Ireland by mythical groups of people. While heavily influenced by Christian historians and scholars, the *Book of Invasions* still reflects the heightened presence of the supernatural in Celtic myth. The first of the four invasions occurred before the time of the biblical Flood and was said to be led by Cesair, the granddaughter of Noah. Cesair was accompanied by fifty women and three men. When the Flood came, within weeks of their arrival, all but one man, Fintan, drowned in the Flood. Fintan, who had magical powers, survived by turning himself into a salmon and swimming in the high waters. The magical Fintan would manage to escape the notice of subsequent invaders by changing his form, appearing as a hawk, for example, or an eagle. Fintan stayed around for centuries, living alone on the island, escaping the notice of an evil group of beings who lived there called the Fomorians. Fintan came to be the keeper of the past and a witness to many significant events.

Several hundred years after the Flood, a second invasion was led by Partholón, who came to Ireland from Greece. Partholón changed the face of Ireland with his magical abilities. He cleared wooded land and created plains, and was said to have invented the process of brewing beer. He even made seven lakes appear where none had been before. Partholón engaged in the first battle on Irish soil when he and his people fought against the evil Fomorians, whose name means "under demons." Despite his special talents, Partholón had not defeated the Fomorians when he and his people were wiped out by a plague.

The next group of invaders was led by Nemhedh. Like Partholón, Nemhedh created landforms in Ireland, but his group, too, was subject to the terror of the Fomorian rule. Nemhedh was defeated, and every year at Halloween the cruel Fomorians forced their subjects to give over two-thirds of their grain and milk and, far worse, two-thirds of their newborn babies as a tax. Fed up, Nemhedh's people fled to Greece. Sometime later, they returned, this time joined by a powerful people called the Fir Bolg who settled Ireland, divided the land into provinces, and set up the system of kingship under a figure they considered to be semidivine. The Fir Bolg were successful and lived a life of prosperity until the next group of magical beings arrived.

The Tuatha Dé Danann and Their Battles

These were the Tuatha Dé Danann, a race of deities who were the children of the goddess Danu, mother of the Irish race, and probably the most significant of the invaders. Writes Timothy R. Roberts in *The Celts in Myth and Legend*, "They may be the mythical reflection of an historical invasion of Ireland about 500 B.C. of people who brought with them the secret of ironworking."[33] Indeed, the Tuatha Dé Danann carried with them from their native Greece four powerful, magic objects to use in their battles against both the Fir Bolg and the Fomorians. In *Druids, Gods, and Heroes*, writer Anne Ross offers this description: "Among these the treasured possessions brought to Ireland by the Tuatha Dé Danann 'were four sacred objects which appear again and again throughout Celtic myths: the Lia Fail, a stone which uttered a shriek at the inauguration of a rightful king; the invincible spear of Lugh; the deadly sword of Nuada; and the ever-plentiful cauldron of the Dagda, the "Good god," the father-god of Ireland.'"[34]

Upon arriving on the shores of Ireland, their first magic tool was to spread darkness around themselves so that they could roam the country undetected as they summed up the forces they would need to conquer. Dagda, the "good god," was the father god of the Tuatha Dé Danann. In battle, he had not only his inexhaustible cauldron that never lacked for food, but also his magic club that could both take and restore life.

Nuadu Loses an Arm

The first battle of the Tuatha Dé in this new land was with the Fir Bolg. In this fight, called the First Battle of Magh Tuiredh, the Nuada, the king of the Tuatha Dé Danann, lost his arm. Because no king could have a physical imperfection, a new king was appointed. Bres, who was half Fomorian, was made king until Nuadu had a new arm made for him by Dian Cécht, the god of healing. After a hard fight, the Tuatha Dé defeated the Fir Bolg, who were forced to live on the Aran Islands off the coast.

The Tuatha Dé had another force to conquer before they could claim Ireland as their own: the evil Fomorians, that ancient group who had successfully fought off the early invaders. The Fomorians were a formidable group, imposing both taxes and punishment on the Tuatha Dé. It was only a matter of time before war broke out. This second conflict for the Tuatha Dé Danann was called the Second Battle of Magh Tuiredh.

The Fomorians were ruled by an evil leader named Balor of the Baleful Eye. A single glance from Balor could mean instant death. Writes Proinsias Mac Cana in *Celtic Mythology*, Balor's eye "was such that it required four men to raise its lid, and when uncovered its venomous gaze could disable an army."[35] In addition to this ability to kill, Balor was a god who could withstand any blow to him. All, that is, but one. An ancient prophecy foretold that he would be killed by his own grandson. But Balor ignored this warning because he did not know that the triplets born to his daughter did not die

After the Fir Bolg and Nemhedh people returned to Ireland they divided the land into provinces and built impressive fortresses like Dun Aengus on Inishmore of the Aran Islands.

when Balor threw them into the sea. One lived and grew up to become a most formidable opponent, the Tuatha Dé Danann god of light, Lugh.

Lugh, the "Shining One"

Part Tuatha Dé Danann on his father's side and Fomorian on his mother's, Lugh played a big role in early Celtic myth. While Balor represented evil, darkness, and thus the Otherworld, Lugh represented goodness and light. In fact, his name means "Shining One." Lugh was also a warrior god with a special connection to the gods of crafts and metalworking, whom he called on to give him magical weapons in battle. Lugh had a magical spear, a boat called *Wavesweeper* that could float through any wave, and the Answerer, a sword that could cut anything. Lugh was also strong on the battlefield, moving his men about with a magical chant. He is famous for his role as a military leader, offering his counsel to Nuadu in his battle against the Fomorians.

Mac Cana, in *Celtic Mythology*, describes Lugh's role in the battle against the Fomorians:

Under Lugh's direction preparations are set on foot and each of the craftsmen and the magicians of the Tuatha Dé promises his own special contribution: the craftsmen to fashion wondrous weapons, the sorcerer to hurl the mountains of Ireland on the Fomhoire [another name for Fomorians], the cupbearer to conceal from them the waters of Ireland's lakes and rivers, the druid to cast upon them three showers of fire, to deprive them of two-thirds of their strength and valour and to bind in their bodies the urine of humans and horses. [36]

It was Lugh who used a slingshot and slew the evil Balor with a single blow to the Fomorian leader's powerful eye.

The battle between these two opposing forces—one representing darkness and evil, the other representing light—resulted in victory for the Tuatha Dé Danann and the banishment of the Fomorians from Ireland. In one version, Balor was not banished but was left to live if he agreed to help the Tuatha Dé with advice about farming and agriculture, which was something the Fomorians were quite skilled at.

A Peaceful World of Immortality

The Tuatha Dé were not to win the next big battle, which was against the Sons of Mil, a group of invaders from Gael (modern Spain) who would give Ireland its ancient name, Hiberia. This group, the first Celts, were to be the permanent inhabitants of Ireland. The Sons of Mil were led by Amhairghin, another warrior with magical powers. When the Tuatha Dé were defeated, they were said to have withheld from the Sons of Mil all corn and milk until an agreement was made. Together, the Tuatha Dé and the Sons of Mil decided to divide the land into two regions: the upper world on earth and the underground.

The Tuatha Dé went to live underground in part of the Otherworld, in mounds of earth called *sidh*, or fairy mounds. Although the *sidhs* were underground, they had green grass and blue skies, and music and food in abundance. It was a peaceful place where living warriors could visit, for feasting and the company of beautiful women. Warriors might even engage in fighting there, a magical kind of fighting that resulted in no lasting wounds. The subterranean Otherworld in early myths was, writes Miranda J. Green in her *Dictionary of Celtic Myth and Legend*, "a magical equivalent of the upper world, with rulers, hierarchies, loves and quarrels. But there was immortality there, agelessness and beauty, and the Tuatha Dé continued to practise their powers of magic and control over the supernatural."[37] In later myths, the heroes would sometimes visit there, accessing it through a cave or lake, or be visited by Otherworld inhabitants. Interestingly, the Otherworld was primarily a positive, happy place for the invited visitor. But for those mythic heroes who arrived uninvited, perhaps in search of something, the Otherworld could be a macabre land of the dead, full of peril and hazards.

Finn mac Cumhaill and His Band of Warriors

Another such warrior with ties to the supernatural was Finn mac Cumhaill, sometimes called Finn Mac Cool. Finn mac Cumhaill was an exceptional figure. From a young age, he displayed impressive supernatural power. His father died when he was young, and he was raised by women warriors in the woods. At the age of eight, he proved himself an able warrior, slaying an evil fire-breathing giant named Aillen mac Midna who, once a year, came to the royal court of Tara, used magical music to put everyone there into a trance, and then burned down the palace. Finn, however, insisted he could kill the evil Aillen mac Midna. When the giant arrived to burn the palace, Finn was ready for him. Finn resisted the spell of sleepiness by pressing the sharp point of a magical spear against his forehead to keep him awake. Alone with the fire-breathing creature, Finn was able to kill and behead him.

Finn was said to have acquired a special wisdom from an experience with a salmon, a fish that holds magical powers in Celtic myth. In this tale, a poet named Finnigas had spent seven years fishing for the Salmon of Knowledge. When Finnigas finally caught it, he gave it to Finn to cook. Finn proceeded to cook it, but burned himself in the process. When he put his finger into his mouth to soothe the burn, he was said to have acquired the power of prophecy. He acquired eternal wisdom when he went on to eat the fish. To access these powers, Finn had only to place his finger into his mouth.

Finn mac Cumhaill was leader of an elite group of warriors called the Fianna. Finn and his warriors roamed Ireland, hunting and fighting and helping to maintain order. Their adventures are thought

The mythical warrior Finn mac Cumhaill (foreground) led the Fianna, an elite group of warriors that helped to maintain social order in Ireland.

to be the basis for the later tales of the Knights of the Round Table of Arthurian legend. To gain entry into this distinguished group, new recruits had to pass a rigorous test. Mac Cana describes it in *Celtic Mythology:*

> Membership of the [Fianna] was highly exclusive, but not hereditary: it could be acquired only by fulfilling certain conditions of admission and by undergoing initiatory ordeals

as proof of exceptional dexterity and prowess. The would-be *féinnidh* [new recruit] was armed with a shield and a hazel stick and placed standing up to his waist in a hole in the ground, and nine warriors cast their spears at him simultaneously. If he suffered hurt thereby he was not accepted into the Fian. Next his hair was braided and he was made to run through the woods of Ireland pursued at a brief interval by all the warriors. If he was overtaken and wounded he was not accepted. Moreover, if his weapons had quivered in his hand, if his hair had been disturbed by a hanging branch, or if a dead branch had cracked under his foot, then neither was he accepted. He had also to leap over a bough as high as his forehead while in full flight and pass under one as low as his knee, and he must be able to draw a thorn from his foot without slackening his pace. Otherwise he was not admitted among the followers of [Finn].[38]

Cú Chulainn and the Cattle Raid of Cooley

Tales of the colorful Finn mac Cumhaill are joined in Celtic myth by another great warrior and hero, Cú Chulainn. Cú

The Magical Power of the Severed Head

The Celtic interest in severed heads is undeniable. The presence of severed heads is noted in grave recovery, in representational art, and in historical accounts. Severed heads play a significant role in the myth as well. Cú Chulainn carries them off the battlefield. Bran the Blessed

loses his head, but it lives on after his body is dead. Lomma, Finn's fool, loses his head, but even mounted on a post, the head still speaks. The pagan Celts believed that the soul inhabited the head in such a fashion that a head could continue to live after decapitation.

Decapitated heads were important trophies of war to the Celts and could be seen mounted on a post, displayed in a warrior's home, hanging from a horse's breast, or even used as drinking cups. In some myths, a severed head is even present on the dining table.

A Gaullish warrior holds up the severed head of his enemy, a very important war trophy to the Celts.

Chulainn's adventures are found in the Ulster cycle, his most famous tale in *The Tain*, or *The Cattle Raid of Cooley*. The main conflict of *The Tain* was a battle between the two regions of Ireland, Connacht and Ulster, over a brown bull named Donn of Cuailnge. The tale begins with the royal couple of Connacht, Queen Medb (also spelled Maeve, Maev, and Medhbh) and King Ailill, fighting over who between them had the most possessions. Queen Medb discovered that she would have been the winner had she still owned the white bull Finnbennach, who had once been hers but who had gone to the king because it did not want to be owned by a woman. To win this contest, the queen decided she must have the brown bull Donn of Cuailnge owned by King Conchobar of Ulster. Queen Medb directed her attention to stealing him.

Queen Medb assembled her army. King Conchobar did the same, asking Cú Chulainn to aid him in the fight. Cú Chulainn, like Finn mac Cumaill, was a superior warrior. Miranda Green, in *Dictionary of Celtic Myth and Legend,* explains how Cú Chulainn, as the "epitome of the superhuman war-hero," shares characteristics with other heroes of Celtic myth. She explains: "Typically, he is destined to have a short, brilliant life covered with glory. He is unsurpassed in battle, young, valorous, of superhuman strength and beautiful. He is closely associated with the gods, and he himself is of supernatural origin." [39]

Cú Chulainn was all these things. In most accounts, he is the son of the god Lugh, but he also had foster fathers, such as the warriors Ferghus and Conall, who led him into the life of a warrior. Like Finn, Cú Chulainn distinguished himself as special at a young age. When he was only seven, Cú Chulainn decided to go to King Conchobar's court and find a position there. On the way, he was confronted by 150 boys who were practicing to become warriors. The boys, looking to provoke the young Cú Chulainn, began attacking him. Cú Chulainn, who was then called by his boyhood name, Setanta, fought back. According to the Kinsella translation:

> They shouted at him, but still he came on against them. They flung three times fifty javelins at him, and he stopped them all on his shield of sticks. Then they drove all their hurling-balls at him, and he stopped every ball on his breast. They threw their hurling-sticks at him, three times fifty of them: he dodged so well that none of them touched him, except for a handful that he plucked down as they shot past. [40]

After that, Cú Chulainn went into the berserk state that he became known for and defeated them soundly. King Conchobar was said to be so impressed that he made Cú Chulainn the young warriors' new leader.

The next challenge earned him his name. Culann, the blacksmith, had a ferocious guard dog who threatened Setanta (Cú Chulainn's given name). In response, the young warrior killed the dog and then

Cú Chulainn Goes Berserk

Cú Chulainn's, "warp spasm" is described in detail in *Táin Bó Cuailnge*. Thomas Kinsella translates in his book, *The Tain*.

The first warp-spasm seized [Cú Chulainn], and made him into a monstrous thing, hideous and shapeless, unheard of. His shanks and his joints, every knuckle and angle and organ from head to foot, shook like a tree in the flood or a reed in the stream. His body made a furious twist inside his skin, so that his feet and shins and knees switched to the rear and his heels and calves switched to the front. The balled sinews of his calves switched to the front of his shins, each big knot the size of a warrior's bunched fist. On his head the temple-sinews stretched to the nape of his neck, each mighty, immense, measureless knob as big as the head of a month-old child. His face and features became a red bowl: he sucked one eye so deep into his head that a wild crane couldn't probe it onto his cheek out of the depths of his skull; the other eye fell out along his cheek. His mouth weirdly distorted: his cheek peeled back from his jaws until the gullet appeared, his lungs and liver flapped in his mouth and throat, his lower jaw struck the upper a lion-killing blow, and fiery flakes large as a ram's fleece reached his mouth from his throat. His heart boomed loud in his breast like the baying of a watch-dog at its feed or the sound of a lion among bears. Malignant mists and spurts of fire . . . flickered red in the vaporous clouds that rose boiling above his head, so fierce was his fury. The hair of his head twisted like the tangle of a red thornbush stuck in a gap; if a royal apple tree with all its kingly fruit were shaken above him, scarce an apple would reach the ground but each would be spiked on a bristle of his hair as it stood up on his scalp with rage. The hero-halo rose out of his brow, long and broad as a warrior's whetstone, long as a snout, and he went mad rattling his shields, urging on his charioteer and harassing the hosts. Then, tall and thick, steady and strong, high as the mast of a noble ship, rose up from the dead centre of his skull a straight spout of black blood darkly and magically smoking.

offered to stand guard in its place, thus earning his name, Cú Chulainn, which means Hound of Culann.

A Magical Warrior

Cú Chulainn was aided in his subsequent challenges by the magical weapons he carried. His father, Lugh, gave him a chariot and horse, both armed with spikes, and,

according to Roberts in *The Celts in Myth and Legend*, "special body armor made of twenty-seven layers of cowhide."[41] He also received from a war goddess a deadly spear called a *gae bolga*. Anne Ross describes it in *The Pagan Celts*: "It made but a single wound when it entered a man's body but it had thirty barbs in it which cut away the flesh when it was removed."[42] In some

Battlefield Lament

A touching part of the *Táin Bó Cuailnge* epic is the death of Ferdia, by the hand of his friend, Cú Chulainn. Both are strong warriors who found themselves on opposite sides of the fight. From *The Tain*, translated by Thomas Kinsella, is Cú Chulainn's heartbroken lament after the killing of his friend.

Ferdia of the hosts
and the hard blows, beloved
golden brooch, I mourn
your conquering arm
and our fostering together,
a sight to please a prince;
your gold-rimmed shield,
your slender sword,
the ring of bright-silver
on your fine hand,
your skill at chess,
your flushed, sweet cheek,
your curled yellow hair
like a great lovely jewel,
the soft leaf-shaped belt
that you wore at your waist.
You have fallen to the Hound,
I cry for it, little calf.
The shield didn't save you
that you brought to the fray.
Shameful was our struggle,
the uproar and grief!
O fair, fine hero
who shattered armies
and crushed them under foot,
golden brooch, I mourn.

Cú Chulainn slays his dear friend Ferdia in the *Táin Bó Cuailnge* epic.

versions, the *gae bolga* was said to inflict wounds that would never heal.

In *The Tain*, Cú Chulainn fought for King Conchobar, becoming the sole fighter in King Conchobar's army after a curse left the other warriors in a trance and unable to fight. This classic tale of a seventeen-year-old boy facing an entire army is, notes Roberts, "an image that continues to inspire the Irish today."[43]

In ensuing battles against Queen Medb's army, Cú Chulainn fought with cunning, using terrorizing tactics, such as sneaking up to make a kill and shooting at long range with his sling shot, to spread fear within King Connacht's troops. In hand-to-hand conflict, Cú Chulainn fought with superhuman intensity, putting himself into a killing trance. Celtic expert Miranda Green describes Cú Chulainn's state:

> He kills huge numbers of Medb's forces single-handed. When the battle-rage is on him, he goes into "warp-spasm", a berserk fit when he can no longer distinguish friend from foe. When berserk, he becomes a monster; his body spins within its skin; his hair stands on end, surrounded by a halo of light; his muscles swell; one eye bulges, the other sinks into his head; his howl causes all the local spirits to howl with him, driving the enemy mad with terror. [44]

After Cú Chulainn fought for four months, the other warriors in the Ulster army healed from their trance and joined the young warrior, who at one sad point in the narrative was forced to fight—and kill—his dear friend and foster brother, Ferdia. The end of this tale has several versions, but all agree on a ferocious battle scene between the two armies that concluded in a battle of the two bulls, the white bull Finnbennach, belonging to King Ailill, and the brown bull Donn of Cuailnge, belonging to King Conchobar.

At the end, the coveted brown bull of King Conchobar was the winner. Victorious, the brown bull carried King Ailill's Finnbennach between his horns, slowly dropping body parts all over Ireland; places such as Finnlethe, meaning White One's Shoulderblade, still bear the bull's name. Once the body was distributed, Donn of Cuailgne dropped dead, the Ridge of the Bull marking the spot. With this battle ended, says Kinsella's *The Tain*, "Ailill and Medb made peace with Ulster and [Cú Chulainn]. For seven years afterward none of their people was killed in Ireland . . . the Connachtmen went back to their own country, and the men of Ulster went back to [the royal court of] Emain Macha full of their great triumph." [45]

Myths such as these tales of Finn mac Cumhaill and Cú Chulainn were part of the rich oral tradition that characterized the Celtic world. Their colorful myths reflect a love and respect for homeland, for life's mysteries and the supernatural, and for music and feasting. The myths, too, celebrate such human qualities as fighting skills, bravery, courage, and loyalty—all values associated with war. The Celtic portrayal of the adventures of the mythic warrior is unsurpassed.

War and Peace in the Wild Land of the Giants

Chapter Four

Norse mythology probably began in the Bronze Age, as early as 1600 B.C., and has its roots in a Germanic race that, like the Celts, migrated across Europe, settling in the northern lands of Scandinavia in Norway, Sweden, and Denmark. During the Viking Age, these seafaring adventurers expanded their territory to Iceland and other lands, plundering shorelines and waterways in their quest for domination. Their mythology reflects the rugged, isolated lifestyle these early sailors must have known in this cold, challenging land.

Much of what is known about Norse myth, or Viking myth as it is also called, comes from two important collections compiled in the thirteenth century. The older collection, the *Poetic Edda*, was thought to have been written by many different poets. The *Poetic Edda* includes the "Voluspa," a significant poem about the creation and end of the world. The other collection, the *Prose Edda*, was compiled by the Icelandic scholar Snorri Sturluson. These medieval works of literature include mythical tales, along with other works of literature. Appearing as they did in the Viking Age, the *Eddas* were influenced by Christianity, and yet they are a valuable presentation of the Norse mythological world of fighting gods and giants.

Fire and Ice

The distinctive climate and lands of Scandinavia are reflected in the creation stories and poems told in the *Eddas*. The natural world of northern Europe included gentle farmland and soft breezes, but it also included more formidable environments such as those found on the cold seas of Norway, along the misty shorelines of the British Isles, and in the frosty plains of Denmark. Iceland, known as the Land of Fire and Ice, was an island with contrasting elements of nature: cold seas, hot springs, and active volcanoes. Therefore, it is not surprising that in Norse myth the world begins with the opposing forces of fire and ice.

According to Norse myth, in the beginning of all time, the universe was divided into two parts: a fire- and light-filled region called Muspellheim in the south, and a cold, dark, and misty northern world called Niflheim. Between the two was a deep chasm called Ginnungap. The hostility between these two opposing worlds began with a spark of fire that leaped across Ginnungap and began to melt the ice of the frozen north. This combination of fire and ice created the first creatures, the frost giant Ymir and a cow, Audumla. The cow began licking at the salt seas, uncovering in the process the first god, Buri.

A Gruesome Beginning

Buri immediately created a son named Bor, and together the pair began to fight their natural enemy, the giants. Notes H. A. Guerber in *Myths of the Norsemen*,

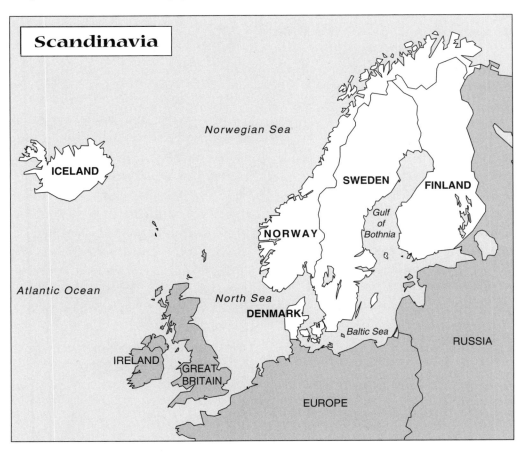

"The gods and giants represented the opposite sides of good and evil, there was no hope of their living together in peace."[46] Then Bor married Besta, the frost giant's daughter, and together they had three sons, Odin, Vili, and Ve. These three warrior gods joined in the war with the giants, succeeding in killing Ymir. From his body the gods created all the parts of the world. Ymir's blood produced the world's rivers and seas. Bor's sons "shaped the earth from Ymir's flesh and the mountains from his unbroken bones; from his teeth and jaws and the fragments of his shattered bones they made rocks and boulders and stones,"[47] writes Kevin Crossley-Holland, in The Norse Myths. After they had formed the earth, they put down a great, rocking ocean that was so wide most men would fear to cross it. The sons continued to form the heavens, using Ymir's skull to make the skies, and the sparks and embers to form the sun and moon and other stars in the sky. Ymir's brains became clouds. The three warrior gods had one additional creation. Using two fallen trees, they created the first humans, Ask and Embla. From this couple, all humans descended. Then Bor's sons took the maggots from the dead body of Ymir and created a little people, the race of dwarfs, gnomes, and trolls.

Mythical Realms

The cosmos was divided into three realms: Asgard, the sky realm of the gods; Midgard, the middle realm of earth; and Niflheim, the underworld. Each realm had three worlds, making nine worlds in all.

The small people were to live in Midgard, which was also inhabited by humans. The remaining giants lived in Midgard, but in a lower region called Jotunheim, the world of the giants. Here a new generation of giants was created from a frost giant, Bergelmir, and his wife, the only two to escape when the sons of Bor killed the giant Ymir.

The gods lived in the highest realm, Asgard, which could be reached by crossing Bifrost, a fiery rainbow. In the beginning, Asgard was a peaceful place where harmony reigned for the gods, who lived in palaces of precious metals. In this golden age of peace, Asgard was home to Odin and the pantheon of gods who were called the Aesir.

Encompassing the nine worlds, which were suspended one above the other, like flattened plates on a mobile, was a magnificent ash tree called Yggdrasil, also called the World Tree. The leaves on Yggdrasil were always green, its trunk and roots always fed with water. Yggdrasil was a symbol of unity, support, and stability against the forces of chaos. It connected all the nine worlds and offered each life-giving nourishment and water. A description of Yggdrasil by P. Grappin in Larousse World Mythology illustrates how the tree, a revered object of nature to this Germanic culture, was a symbol of both harmony and discord:

> There are many animals living in the branches of the great ash-tree: at the very top a gold cock scans the

Words from an Ancient Prophecy

In one of the poems in the collection called the *Poetic Edda*, translated by Carolyne Larrington, the seer in the *Seeress's Prophecy* presents the mythical story of creation. She describes the end of the world and the new golden age that will come, suggesting, perhaps, that the evil "dark dragon" may still be about.

She sees, coming up a second time,
Earth from the ocean, eternally green;
the waterfall plunges, an eagle soars over it,
hunting fish on the mountain.

The Æsir meet on Idavoll
and they converse about the mighty Earth-girdler,
and they remember there the great events
and the ancient runes of the Mighty One.

There afterwards will be found in the grass
the wonderful golden chequers,
those which they possessed in the ancient times.

Without sowing the fields will grow,
all ills will be healed, Baldr will come back;
Hod and Baldr, the gods of slaughter, will live happily together
in the sage's palaces—do you understand yet, or what more?

Then Hænir will choose wooden ships for prophecy,
and the sons of two brothers will inhabit, widely,
the windy world—do you understand yet, or what more?

A hall she sees standing, fairer than the sun,
thatched with gold, at Gimle;
there the noble lords will live
and spend their days in pleasure.

Then the powerful, mighty one, he who rules over everything,
will come from above, to the judgement-place of the gods.

There comes the dark dragon flying,
the shining serpent, up from Dark-of-moon Hills;
Nidhogg flies over the plain, in his wings
he carries corpses; now she must sink down.

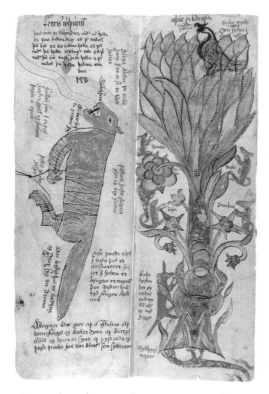

Pictured on this page from a seventeenth-century Icelandic manuscript is the Yggdrasil, the mythological ash tree binding earth, hell, and heaven together.

horizon and has to warn the gods when their eternal enemies, the giants, prepare to attack them; an eagle surveys the entire world, and between its eyes is perched a hawk; a squirrel named Ratatosk never stops darting up and down the branches between the eagle at the top of the tree and the serpent-dragon at the foot and keeps them in a constant state of discord; a goat called Heidrun feeds on the leaves, and its milk provides food for Odin's warriors; four stags

devour the foliage and even the bark of the tree, which would fail to survive were it not for the water from the magic fountain infusing new life into its veins. Finally, serpents eat away at the roots, particularly the frightening Nidhoggr, which is also described as a dragon on some occasions. [48]

An Uneasy Truce

However, even Yggdrasil could not keep perfect harmony in Asgard, Midgard, and the underworld, Niflheim. The first real war in this new universe occurred between the warlike sky gods of Aesir and another group of gods, the peace-loving Vanir who lived in Vanaheim, another land on Asgard. Unlike the warlike gods of the Aesir, headed by Thor and Odin, the gods of Vanir were associated with prosperity and rich harvest. The three principal Vanir gods were Freyja, goddess of love and rebirth; Freyr, god of peace; and Njord, god of the plentiful sea. The Vanir wished to become a part of the Aesir abode at Asgard.

Different myths explain the sequence of events leading to the war between the two groups, but in one tale, the conflict between these two families of gods began with a witch named Gullveig. Gullveig, who loved gold, was sent to the Aesir. When Odin greeted her and found that all she could talk about was gold, he and the other Aesir quickly grew tired of her. They stabbed and tortured her and then burned her with fire. However, Gullveig was not so easily killed. With her powers of sorcery, she was able to be reborn.

When the Vanir heard of how the Aesir had rejected Gullveig, they became angry and vowed revenge. Even though they were peaceful gods, they prepared for battle. When Odin, all-seeing chief god of the Aesir, saw what they were doing, he thrust his spear, signaling the outbreak of war.

Both the Aesir and Vanir fought hard, using rocks, mountains, and chunks of ice as weapons. After some time, neither the Aesir nor the Vanir had gained a clear advantage. Finally, both sides tired of fighting and began instead to talk. They called a truce and agreed that rather than fight, they would make peace. As proof that the fighting was over, they agreed to exchange leaders. The Vanir's Njord, Freyja, and Freyr went to live in Asgard, while the Aesir's Honir and Mimir went to live in Vanaheim with the Vanir. This exchange worked at first, but then the Vanir grew distrustful. They began to suspect that Honir and Mimir could not make independent decisions and that when Mimir was separated from Honir, Honir could not think on his own. Angry that the Aesir had sent them two gods who could only think when they were together, the Vanir cut off Mimir's head and returned it to Odin. Odin knew that Mimir's head still retained his wisdom. So

An Unusual Truce

In the *Snorri Sturluson Edda,* translated from Icelandic by Anthony Faulkes, the god of poetry, Bragi, explains to Aegir, god of the sea, how poetry came about at the time of the truce between the Vanir and the Aesir. Aegir begins the dialogue:

How did this craft that you call poetry originate?

Bragi replied: "The origin of it was that the gods had a dispute with the people called Vanir, and they appointed a peace-conference and made a truce by this procedure, that both sides went up to a vat and spat their spittle into it. But when they dispersed, the gods kept this symbol of truce and decided not to let it be wasted, and out of it made a man. His name was Kvasir, he was so wise that no one could ask him any questions to which he did not know the answer. He travelled widely through the world teaching people knowledge, and when he arrived as a guest to some dwarfs, Fialar and Galar, they called him to a private discussion with them and killed him. They poured his blood into two vats and a pot, and the latter was called Odrerir, but the vats were called Son and Bodn. They mixed honey with the blood and it turned into the mead whoever drinks from which becomes a poet or scholar. The dwarfs told the Æsir that Kvasir had suffocated in intelligence because there was no one there educated enough to be able to ask him questions."

Odin preserved the head in herbs and kept it near him. Mimir's head could still speak to Odin, and his wise words were a great gift.

Odin, God of War

Odin was a powerful figure in Norse myth. One of the original sons who formed Midgard from the body of the frost giant Ymir, Odin had roots in the Germanic god Woden and was a god of war as well as the all-knowing god of the sky and air. Also called Allfather, Odin sat in a throne and kept an eye on the entire universe. H.A. Guerber, in *Myths of the Norsemen*, describes this significant figure:

> Odin was generally represented as a tall, vigorous man, about fifty years of age, either with dark curling hair or with a long grey beard and bald head. He was clad in a suit of grey, with a blue hood, and his muscular body was enveloped in a wide blue mantle flecked with grey—an emblem of the sky with its fleecy clouds. In his hand Odin generally carried the infallible spear Gungnir, which was so sacred that an oath sworn upon its point could never be broken, and on his finger or arm he wore the marvelous ring, Draupnir, the emblem of fruitfulness, precious beyond compare. When seated upon his throne or armed for the fray . . . Odin wore his eagle helmet; but when he wandered peacefully about the earth in human guise, to see what men were doing, he generally

donned a broad-brimmed hat, drawn low over his forehead to conceal the fact that he possessed but one eye. [49]

Odin was accompanied by two ravens who perched on his shoulders and brought

Odin, depicted in this bronze figurine, was the omniscient Norse god of war, the sky, and the air.

Contrasting Roles for Odin's Valkyries

Valkyries had a special role in Norse myth. These female supernatural figures were servants to Odin. In times of peace, they hung around Valhalla, bringing food and drink to the gods. In times of war, they donned weapons and armor and flew to the battlefield. Invisible to the warriors, the valkyries could choose who would die and who would survive the fighting. When a fighter was dead, the valkyrie would carry the corpse back to Asgard. Because of this battlefield presence, valkyries were associated with blood and carnage.

him news of the world. At his feet were two wolves, Geri and Freki. In war, Odin rode an eight-footed horse named Sleipnir, and carried a white shield and a magic bow that could shoot ten arrows at once.

Valhalla, Home to Fallen Warriors

Odin was loved by warriors. Observes Guerber, "The ancient Northern nations, who deemed warfare the most honorable of occupations, and considered courage the greatest virtue, worshiped Odin principally as god of battle and victory."[50] They believed that Odin had a palace called Valhalla where warriors who had fallen in battle were rewarded. Decorated with the weapons of war—shiny spears on the roof of the mansion, a great hallway lined with shields—Valhalla was a fitting reward for the courageous who had met their death on the battleground.

When the fallen arrived, they were greeted and praised for their courage by Odin. Then they were given a great feast with all the mead they could drink and platters of boar meat that never emptied. But there were greater rewards as well. After they ate, they armed themselves for

fighting and went to the courtyard where they practiced their feats. As in Celtic myth, the wounds of the warriors were not lasting. Thus, Valhalla was a paradise for fighters, a peaceful place of plentiful food and drink and fighting that carried only the honor and none of the tragedy of real war.

The Strength of Thor

Another early Norse god who possessed almost as much power as Odin was the thunder god Thor. Unlike war god Odin, Thor stood for order. The son of Odin and his wife Frigga, Thor was a popular god and a friend to the common people, particularly the farmers, who called on him to control the weather and to fight off the frost giants with their cold, crop-destroying winds. The sound of thunder was said to be caused by the wheels of his goat-drawn chariot. Thor's chief weapon was his huge hammer, Mjolnir. Mjolnir could crush and destroy and magically return itself to Thor's hand. If armed with a second weapon, his magic belt, Thor could throw his hammer twice as far.

Despite Thor's strength, he could not defeat every opponent, as illustrated by

The thunder god Thor wields his hammer Mjolnir and drives his goat-drawn chariot. Thor was extremely popular with the common people, who looked to him for protection.

the tale in which he visited the world of the frost giants. The story began with Thor deciding to go to the land of Jotunheim, where the giants lived, to force them to quit ruining the blossoms and crops with their icy winds. There, Thor confronted the giant king Utgard-Loki. The two faced off in a series of contests, but the giants used their powerful magic to win. For example, in a drinking challenge, the giants connected the ocean to the drinking horn Thor was trying to empty. In another, Thor was challenged to lift the giant's cat, but the cat, unbeknownst to Thor, was in reality the terrible Midgard Serpent, which wrapped itself around the world. Even Thor's blows from his hammer would not work in the land of the frost giants when the giant Utgard-Loki used invisible mountains to shield himself.

Still, the giants were surprised at how well Thor had performed. Writes Crossley Holland, Utgard-Loki told Thor that when "you drank from that horn you thought you were found wanting. But I tell you, I could scarcely believe my eyes. You didn't realise the other end of the horn was in the sea. When you get back to the ocean, you'll see just how much it has ebbed."[51] Thor was angry and lifted his hammer once again, but the giant made his castle disappear, and Thor was left alone on an empty plain. He had no choice but to leave the land of the giants without having conquered them or their evil ways.

Tyr and the Giant Wolf, Fenrir

Tyr, another warrior god of the Aesir, faced a powerful opponent, Fenrir, a giant wolf. The son of Odin and Frigga, Tyr was the god of courage, a quality often associated with war. Writes H.R. Ellis Davidson in *Scandinavian Mythology,* Tyr was a god for warriors: "He ruled the realm of the sky as well as that of battle. . . . Men turned to him for help in war and put his initial, the runic sign for "T", on weapons in the early Ango-Saxon period."[52]

The story most told about Tyr is "The Binding of Fenrir." Fenrir, a giant wolf, was one of the monster children of Utgard-Loki, who himself had descended from the giants. In Norse myth, wolves are danger-

ous beasts, more often than not the winners of conflicts. This wolf, Fenrir, had enjoyed a life of some privilege because rather than being cast from Asgard as all other wolves had been, Odin had let him stay, hoping that the wolf would become tamed and gentle.

But Fenrir grew larger and became more and more threatening. The gods at Asgard decided that he needed to be restrained. When Fenrir broke several different chains the gods had used to bind him, something special needed to be done. The gods resorted to magic, calling on the elves to create a magic ribbon. Peter Andreas Munch describes this special creation in *Norse Mythology: Legends of Gods and Heroes.* The elves "made a chain from the sound of a cat's footfall, the beard of a woman, the roots of a mountain, the sinews of a bear, the breath of fishes, and the spittle of birds; this is the reason why the footfall of the cat no longer has any sound, why women have no beards, why mountains have no roots."[53]

Having broken the other chains, Fenrir was fairly certain he could cast off this slender ribbon as well. But just to be sure, he requested that one of the Aesir place a hand in his mouth as a sign that they could be trusted. The only god brave enough to do so was Tyr, who boldly thrust his hand into the wolf's powerful mouth. When the magic ribbon began to tighten under the wolf's struggling, the beast responded by biting off Tyr's right hand.

The Aesir attached the ribbon to a large slab of rock and Fenrir remained tied. Unable to break the restraint, the wolf was most unhappy. His howls were so piercing that the gods thrust a sword into his mouth. The blood that drained out formed a river called Von. Fenrir was such a threat that he remained in chains until the end of the world when he would be free to seek revenge. In the meantime, the sacrifice of Tyr's hand was what kept the home of the gods safe from Fenrir, at least until the time of the final battle.

The Fall of a Peaceful God

Before this final battle at the end of the world, a destructive war called Ragnarok, a sequence of events between the gods and the forces of evil, took place. The main event that put into motion the end of the world created with the slaying of Ymir was the death of the peaceful, good god named Balder.

In this sixth-century bronze relief, Tyr, the god of courage, battles Fenrir the giant wolf. Tyr sacrificed his right hand to subdue the great beast.

Balder was the Aesir god of sun and light. He was incapable of evil. Balder was the brother of Hodur, a blind god, the god of darkness. Writes Guerber, "Balder, the beautiful, was worshiped as the pure and radiant god of innocence and light. From his snowy brow and golden locks seemed to radiate beams of sunshine which gladdened the hearts of gods and men, by whom he was equally beloved."[54]

But this god of lightness grew dark and solemn when he began to have dreams of his own death. His mother, Odin's wife Frigga, had the power to prevent harm to come to her child. As the powerful wife of the powerful Allfather, Frigga could have everything in creation promise not to harm her innocent and peaceful son. Everything in the universe—rocks, flowers, animals—were part of this vow, all but one single plant, the mistletoe that grew at the gate of Valhalla. Frigga was certain that this insignificant plant would not be a problem. Odin, Balder's father, needed more promise. He visited a seer who suggested that his son would die, but Odin let himself be persuaded by his wife's confidence.

Life went on for the gods and they engaged in their usual leisurely pastimes, until one day they took part in a playful game directed at Balder. Knowing that all manner of inanimate and animate objects in the universe had sworn not to harm Balder, the gods amused themselves by tossing things at the god.

But the evilness of one god could not be stopped. Loki, a devious trickster god, could not resist the temptation to stir things up. He knew that the mistletoe had not made a vow, and he took a branch of it and handed it to Balder's brother, Hodur. Hodur, in his innocence, threw the branch at his brother and Balder fell to the ground, killed by the mistletoe.

Frigga begged the other gods to hurry to the world of the dead and secure the release of her beloved son, Balder. The god Hermod agreed to do it. In Niflheim, Hermod found Balder sitting with Hel, the god of the dead. Hel agreed to release Balder, but only if everything in the world would mourn for Balder. That seemed an easy feat, but little did Hermod know that everything in the world save one giantess named Thok would comply. And so Thok, thought by many scholars to be the evil Loki in disguise, prevented the return of Balder.

The Banishment of Loki and the Destruction of the World

After Balder's death, the events that led to the final battle on earth were set in motion. Loki was banished from Asgard and sent to the middle earth, Midgard, home of the humans. On earth, Loki continued to upset the peace and corrupt men. Writes Munch, "For the space of three years the earth is filled with strife and wickedness; brother kills brother for gain's sake, and the son spares not his own father."[55] This was followed by three more years in which the world grew cold and snowy, as the sun quit warming the earth and the wind blew fiercely. The wolves, said to be chasing the sun and moon through the sky, finally overtook them, and the wounds from the wolves' teeth caused blood to flood the earth.

Munch describes the destruction of the universe. The "heavens and the air are sprayed with blood. The stars are quenched. The earth and all the mountains tremble; trees are uprooted; all bonds are burst asunder. Both Loki and the [Fenrir] Wolf shake off their shackles. The Midgard Serpent, seeking to reach dry lands, swims with such turbulent force that the seas wash over their banks." [56]

The Final Battle

Both sides readied themselves for a battle that would be fought near Valhalla. Loki led the dragon and the Hel-hound Garm, along with the fire-giant Surtr with his burning sword and the frost giants. The gods in Asgard knew their defenses were weak against the evil forces that crossed the bridge of Bifrost and advanced toward them. Writes Guerber, "Nevertheless, the Æsir did not show any signs of despair, but, like true battle-gods of the North, they donned their richest attire, and gaily rode to the battlefield, determined to sell their lives as dearly as possible." [57] The noise of the battle between the two opposing sides filled the universe, and the "gods and giants slay[ed] one another in boundless confusion," [58] notes Grappin.

On the battlefront Odin faced off against Fenrir, the wolf. Thor's challenger

was, once again, the Midgard Serpent. Tyr's opponent was the Hel-hound Garm. But the Aesir gods were no match for these evil monsters and giants, and one by one the gods were killed. Odin, the Allfather, after a hard battle with Fenrir, was one of the first to fall. Thor managed to kill the Midgard Serpent, but died anyway from the monster's venom. The other gods followed until the universe was caught up in a raging flame that destroyed it. The end of the world, Ragnarok, had come.

Peace and Regeneration

However, all was not lost. The Norse believed, writes Guerber,

in regeneration, and held that after a certain space of time, the earth, purged by fire and purified by its immersion in the sea, rose again in all its pristine beauty and was illumined by the sun, whose chariot was driven by a daughter of Sol, born before the wolf had devoured her mother. The new orb of day was not perfect, as the first sun had been, and its rays were no longer so ardent that a shield had to be placed between it and the earth. These more beneficent rays soon caused the earth to renew its green mantle, and to bring forth flowers and fruit in abundance. [59]

While this final battle had been going on, two humans had been sleeping undis-

A stone carving depicts Loki, a mischievous Norse god who delights in creating trouble for his fellow gods.

turbed in the great tree Yggdrasil. They woke up, oblivious to the destruction of the old world, and emerged into a new, green land of peace. As for the gods themselves, the few that remained lived in a heaven that had not been destroyed, a place called Gimli.

The great drama of Norse mythology begins with the creation of the world and ends with its final destruction and rebirth.

While conflicts such as good versus evil, or destruction followed by peaceful rebirth, are not uncommon themes in myth, the characters and circumstances presented in Norse mythology are unique. Odin the Allfather, the trickster Loki, the powerful wolf Fenrir and the magic ribbon, and even the distinctive arrangement of the nine worlds are ingenious inventions by this spirited culture of the north.

Vishnu and Other Demon-Fighters of Hindu Myth

Chapter Five

The mythology of India has its roots in the peaceful agricultural settlements of the Indus River Valley. Over the course of five thousand years, various invading cultures contributed to a far more complex mythology that encompasses hundreds, some say millions, of gods, goddesses, and demons. The great myths of Hinduism were recorded in the *Vedas* of 1000 B.C., followed by the epics *Mahabharata* and the *Ramayana,* and, finally, the *Puranas,* dated at A.D. 300 to 1200. Many of the myths tell of warrior gods and goddesses who assume various forms as they battle evil demons intent on destruction.

Early Gods of the Indus Valley

The mythology of the earliest settlers in the Indus Valley region was far less complex than the Hindu myths that evolved

over time. As early as 3000 B.C., peaceful farmers of the Mohenjo-daro and Harappan settlements lived in orderly cities on the banks of the Indus River. Since they farmed cotton and raised goats, pigs, and sheep, their myths emphasized fertility goddesses and animal deities. Uninterrupted by invaders, this agricultural society prospered for over one thousand years. With the arrival of Aryan tribes from eastern Europe sometime between 3000 and 1500 B.C., the mythology of this region began to change.

The Aryans were warriors who brought with them an array of weaponry, including horse-drawn chariots and finely crafted metal swords. While the earlier farming societies worshiped feminine fertility goddesses, the Aryan deities were male gods of the air and sky. The oldest of Hindu works, the *Vedas,* tell of powerful Vedic deities who established a place in the universe by a show of strength and might against opponents who wished to create chaos.

The major Vedic deity was Varuna, Prime Mover of the universe, as he was often called. In the hierarchal pantheon of Vedic gods, Varuna was at the top, wielding his power from a palace in the sky. Varuna was both a moral leader and a punishing god. He was often portrayed carrying a rope, which he used to tie up those who failed to honor his laws. Over time, Varuna's role diminished.

Fighting the Drought Demon

A rival to Varuna was the demon-fighter Indra, a storm god who carried a thunderbolt in his right hand. A violent god

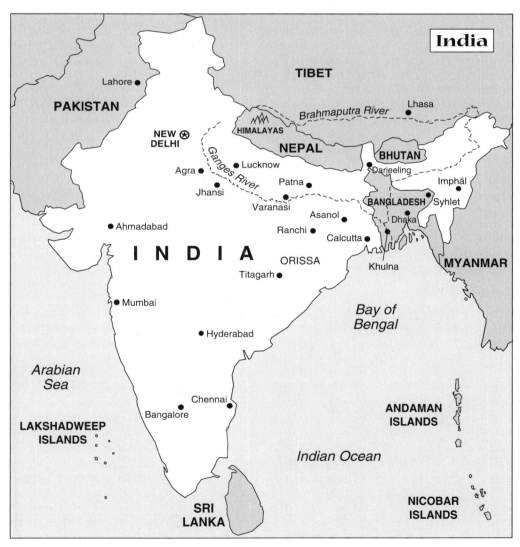

of rains, he was known as the king of gods. Writes Veronica Ions in *Indian Mythology*, "Like an Aryan warrior-king, he is fair-complexioned with ruddy or golden skin and rides a horse, or alternatively rides in a golden chariot drawn by two tawny horses with flowing manes and tails. He has a violent nature, an insatiable thirst for soma, an intoxicating drink which gives him his strength, and is a firm defender of gods and humans against Vritra, a demon who typifies the harsh aspect of nature, especially drought."[60]

A popular myth about Indra tells the story of his encounter with drought demon Vritra. In a fierce battle, Indra took on Vritra, destroying all of his ninety-nine fortresses and demolishing the demon with his thunderbolt. This victory gave Indra power and cemented his position over Varuna. As a warrior god who would engage in fighting to bring forth rain, Indra was highly significant to the people of northern India. This shift in power from Varuna to Indra also reflected a change in Hindu thought. Explains Ions, Indra "stands for the power of personal intervention, for the activity of the warrior, whereas Varuna stands for the inevitability of the cosmic order."[61] Over time Indra began to acquire the role of a fertility god as well.

Sometimes Vedic gods were both friend and foe to humans. Agni, god of fire, for instance, was revered for providing each household with warmth and the means for cooking. Fire was also a destructive force, and in myth Agni destroys entire villages. Likewise, storm god Rudra, sometimes said

to be a form of Agni, had opposing sides to his personality. On the one hand, Rudra, known also as the Howler, could strike fear with his arrows of death. On the other hand, he was clearly a benevolent god who was lord of cattle and music, and a physician who was seen as a healer. Later both Agni and Rudra came to be associated with the Hindu god Shiva.

Brahma, the Creator

Shiva is one of the gods recognized in Hinduism as part of the Triad, or Trimurti. This Triad of the gods Brahma, Vishnu, and Shiva make up the eternal creative force in the universe called Brahman. Together, these three gods embody *sat*, or "that which is." The three, in their different manifestations, represent the complementary forces of creation and destruction that the Hindus believe are needed to achieve balance in the universe. Generally, Brahma is seen as the Creator, Vishnu as the Preserver, and Shiva as the Destroyer.

Numerous myths relate how the deity Brahma created himself and the universe. In some tellings, he created himself from his own will. Then, when he breathed out, the universe was created, and when he breathed in, the universe was destroyed. The time between breaths was two billion years, during which human souls were born and reborn eighty-two thousand times on their path to the Ultimate Reality, the state of Brahman. Brahma is said to represent the balance between the opposing forces of Shiva and Vishnu.

A Cambodian sandstone sculpture depicts Brahma, creator of the universe, one of the Triad of Hindu gods.

Shiva, God of Destruction

Like the Vedic god Rudra, Shiva was capable of great destruction, and yet he was also protective. He was associated with cosmic destruction, but also with the re-creation of the universe that would follow. He was a quarrelsome god who often argued with the other gods, but he was also a benevolent god of hunting, protector of warriors, and ruler of the class in society called the Untouchables.

His physical representation reflected this dual role. His three eyes symbolized the sun, the moon, and destructive fire. His four hands are often depicted holding objects that represent his opposing natures. For example, one hand may be holding fire or a trident to symbolize destruction. In contrast, another hand may hold a drum, symbolizing the order of the universe. Shiva is often portrayed as dancing to the motion of the cosmos.

In one popular myth, Shiva came to the rescue of the other gods in a struggle against the demons. The gods had decided to create a special potion to give them immortality. To create the potion, they used the serpent Vasuki to churn a great ocean called the Ocean of Milk. Vasuki

Shiva and his wife Parvati sit on their throne atop the sacred bull. Shiva and Parvati are Hindu deities of destruction and regeneration.

got dizzy from all the churning and vomited poison. Just when the poison was about to fall into the ocean and make it deadly for the gods, Shiva quickly came to the rescue and swallowed the poison himself, his throat turning blue in the process. He would have died if his wife, Parvati, had not strangled him, which kept the poison in his mouth. Shiva is sometimes pictured with snakes on his arms and neck, symbolizing his power over this deadly reptile and other mysterious creatures of the wild.

Shiva's Multifaceted Wife

Like Shiva, his wife, Parvati, assumed contrasting personalities. Probably a remnant of the fertility goddesses of the Indus Valley, Shiva's wife appeared in various forms, as consorts to all the gods of the Triad. Known as Mahadevi Shakti, Sati, Durga, Kali, and Lakshami, she represented the two extremes of order and destruction. She was a sweet maiden and model wife, but she could also take the form of a ferocious demon.

Parvati was a fierce fighter who rode a tiger and carried in her ten hands an assortment of weapons, including Shiva's trident, Vishnu's discus, and Indra's thunderbolt. Her first opponent was the buffalo-demon Mahisha, who attacked her in many different manifestations but could not defeat the goddess, who eventually killed him with a spear.

Before taking Durga's name from him, Shiva's wife fought the demon. Durga had enormous powers of destruction. Ions writes in *Indian Mythology* that "rivers changed their courses, fire lost its strength and the stars disappeared. Durga pervaded all the natural world, producing rain when he wished and forcing the earth to bear heavy crops even out of season."[62] Shiva's wife was called in and battled against the demon, with its army of "100,000,000 chariots, 120,000,000,000 elephants, 10,000,000 horses and innumerable soldiers."[63] But she had special powers of her own. In this mighty battle, she grew one thousand arms and produced 9 million beings from her own body to aid her in the fight. Durga threw a mountain at her, but she split it into seven pieces. Durga grew to the size of an elephant but was still no match for the goddess fighter. Even when Durga became the size of a buffalo, Shiva's wife was able to defeat him. Finally, she pierced him through the breast with a spear and he died. In victory, she took his name.

Vishnu, the Restorer

Like Shiva, Vishnu was originally a minor god, associated with Indra, the Aryan war god. Vishnu was a beloved member of the Triad who was worshiped for his benevolence and for his role as preserver. In paintings and other artwork, Vishnu was often depicted as a handsome, princelike figure, seen with his wife, Lakshami. In Vishnu's four hands are a conch to announce victory in war; a discus, a weapon given to him by the god Indra; a club, representing his royal power; and a lotus, symbolizing

Durga Slays the Buffalo Demon

The buffalo demon is no match for the goddess Durga, particularly after she drinks her "supreme wine," the blood of her victims. This excerpt is from *Hindu Myths*, translated by Wendy Doniger O'Flaherty.

Then the great demon once more assumed his buffalo shape and shook the triple world, moving and still. Enraged by this, the furious mother of the universe drank the supreme wine again and again; her eyes became red, and she laughed. The demon roared, puffed up and intoxicated with his own strength and courage, and with his two horns he hurled mountains at the furious Goddess, but she pulverized his missiles with a hail of arrows.

Then she spoke to him, her syllables confused with passion as they tumbled from her mouth which was loosened by intoxication. The Goddess said, "Roar and roar for a moment, you fool, while I drink this honeyed wine. The gods will soon roar when I have slain you here." Then she leaped up and mounted that great demon and kicked him in the neck with her foot and pierced him with her trident. When he was struck by her foot he came halfway out of his own mouth, for he was enveloped in the Goddess's heroic power. And as the great demon came halfway out, fighting, the Goddess cut off his head with his great sword, and he fell. Thus the demon named Buffalo was destroyed by the Goddess, together with his army and her band of friends, when he had bewitched the triple world. And when the buffalo had fallen, all the creatures in the triple world, along with all the gods and demons and men, shouted, "Victory!" A cry of lamentation arose from the entire demon army as it was destroyed, and all the bands of gods rejoiced. Then the gods and the heavenly great sages praised the Goddess, the Gandharva leaders sang, and the bands of celestial nymphs danced.

creativity. Vishnu was often seen riding Garuda, an eaglelike sunbird who acted as Vishnu's messenger.

Vishnu's role among the gods was to maintain balance in the universe—between order and disorder, between good and evil. Unlike Brahma and Shiva, Vishnu was not concerned with his ranking in the Triad. He was a patient god but a powerful one who was called on to come to earth and fight demons who were threatening humanity. As the restorer of law and order, Vishnu appeared in at least ten different forms or personalities. In each of these incarnations, called avatars, Vishnu restored harmony and balance.

Sometimes Vishnu was reincarnated as an animal. As a fish, he helped save humankind from the great flood. As a tortoise, Vishnu dove to the bottom of the ocean and found a valuable potion that the gods needed to achieve immortality. As a boar, Vishnu rescued the earth after the demon Hiranyaksha tossed it to the bottom of the sea. In his fourth animal form, a half-human half-lion, Vishnu battled the demon Hiranyakashapa, who ruled over the entire earth and had a deep hatred for Vishnu. Hiranyakashapa, it was said, could be killed by neither human nor animal, neither inside nor outside, and neither at day or at night. To outsmart the demon, Vishnu took the form of a half-lion half-human and killed the demon at dusk in the doorway of his home.

In another incarnation, this time as a human, Vishnu was able to outsmart the demon Bali. When demon-king Bali seized control of the world, Vishnu, in the form of a dwarf, approached him and asked, "Will you give me control over all the earth I can cover with three strides?" The king agreed, assuming a dwarf would not cover much ground. But Vishnu contained the entire universe in his body. As related in Wendy Doniger O'Flaherty's *Hindu Myths*: "But the dwarf, the lord, stepped over the heaven, the sky, and earth, this whole universe, in three strides; he, the famous one, the individual soul, surpassed the sky in his own energy, illuminating all the regions of the sky and the intermediate points of the compass. The great-armed [Vishnu] who excites men shone forth, illuminating all the world, and stole away the demons' prosperity as he stole away the three worlds."[64] Vishnu gave the new kingship of the land to the god Indra.

Vishnu in the Epic Poem, *Ramayana*

Vishnu's next task was to free the earth of the powerful ruling class of Kshatriyas and restore power to the priests. To do so, Vishnu took the form of both warrior and holy man. *Ramayana*, the epic poem, tells

Vishnu adopted several avatars, or incarnations, to work for the benefit of humanity. Here, Vishnu, in the form of Rama, rescues his earthly wife Sita from Ravana, the demon-king.

of the many adventures of Vishnu in his two incarnations of a Rama-figure: Parasurama and then Ramachandra, or Rama for short. The epic *Ramayana* begins with a test of Parasurama's devotion to his father, Jamadagni, and ends with Ramachandra's battle with the ten-headed demon-king, Ravana. After Parasurama's father discovered that his wife, Parasurama's mother, had been having impure thoughts after witnessing a young couple in a moment of privacy, Jamadagni ordered his sons to kill their mother by beheading her. Each son refused—all but Parasurama, who carried out his father's command and beheaded his own mother. Pleased with his son's obedience, Jamadagni granted his son two wishes. Parasurama asked to be unbeatable in single combat and that his mother's life be restored. Both wishes were granted.

Parasurama's special strengths served him well in the battle that came next. A powerful king named Kartavirya stole a cow from Parasurama's father, and Parasurama was sent to seek revenge. But when he killed the king and returned home afterward, he found his dear father dead. Parasurama's anger turned toward the caste of Kartavirya. In anger, he killed the entire caste: "All their menfolk were exterminated, their blood filling five large lakes,"[65] writes Ions in *Indian Mythology*. With the ruling caste out of power and the power of the gods and the holy Brahman restored, Parasurama retreated to the mountains to live in peace.

Rama Battles the Ten-Headed Demon-King

In his incarnation of Rama, Vishnu fought the demon-king Ravana who had achieved too much power. Ravana had captured some of the gods and taken them to Sri Lanka where he had chained them and

The Maruts

The Maruts were wind gods who were warrior storm gods. They fought alongside Indra in this storm god's constant battles with the demon Vritra, god of drought. Veronica Ions offers this lively description of the Maruts in *Indian Mythology*.

They were handsome young men, vigorous and courageous, who, according to the Rig Veda, numbered either twenty-seven or one hundred and eighty. They wore golden helmets and golden breastplates and they draped bright skins on their shoulders. . . . When they rode forth they "rode on the whirlwind and directed the storm," and were conveyed on a golden-wheeled chariot sparkling in the lightning and drawn by three fleet-footed deer. They were strongly armed with bows and arrows and axes, and especially with gleaming spears. With these weapons they shattered the cloud-cattle and cleft cloud-rocks, so that torrents of rain fell to earth and the eye of the sun was covered.

The monkey god Hanuman (left) leads an army of monkeys and men into battle against the forces of Ravana.

made them his servants. The gods were helpless in fighting Ravana because Brahma had granted him a special immunity from being harmed by a god. So Vishnu agreed to take the form of a human who would do battle with the most powerful demon the gods had known. Rama appeared on earth as the son of King Dasratha. When Dasratha stepped down from the throne, he wished for Rama to take his place, but he had promised his queen that a different son would rule. In keeping with that promise, Rama, along with his princess bride, Sita, was exiled to the forest, despite the wishes of this brother not to serve in Rama's place.

With this exile the troubles began for Rama. In the forest, Rama, Sita, and another brother, Lakshamana, began to have confrontations with the demon-king's sister, Surpanakha. Surpanakha first fell in love with Rama and then with Lakshamana, but they both spurned her. Angry at being rejected, Surpanakha went home to her brother the demon-king and began to stir up more trouble, telling stories of Sita's beauty until the demon-king wanted Rama's wife for himself.

To capture her, the demon-king knew he had to use trickery. So he sent a magic deer into the forest to distract the two brothers. While they chased it, the demon-king grabbed Sita and took her with him to his palace in Sri Lanka, wounding a bird friend of Rama's on the way out of the woods. When Rama and his brother returned and discovered that Sita was gone, they knew it was time to battle the demon-king. To do so, Rama enlisted the help of the general of the monkey army, a flying monkey god named Hanuman, who was also the son of Vayu, the wind god. Rama was correct to be confident in Hanuman.

The monkey god easily reached Ravana's palace, found Sita, and gave her Rama's ring with the promise that her husband would soon rescue her. But Hanuman was captured and brought before the demon-king. The demon-king knew his opponent, Hanuman. To kill him quickly, he ordered that oily cloth be wrapped around Hanuman's tail and set on fire. This was done, but Hanuman escaped and scurried around the palace grounds, setting fire to the buildings before flying back to Rama and Lakshamana. The two brothers gathered their army of monkeys and returned to the palace gates.

The battle between the demons and the monkey army began. All the demons were killed except for the demon-king Ravana. Rama and Ravana engaged in hand-to-hand combat. Rama pulled out his magic weapon and shot it from his bow. Ravana dropped to the ground and died. Following this war, the earth experienced a period of peace.

Vishnu, as Krishna

Vishnu, in the form of Krishna, was the chief deity in the epic poem, the *Mahabharata*. Krishna, like Vishnu in other avatars, worked to restore order to a mythical world that was out of control. This chaos was brought on by a war between two families. The five Pandava brothers, who were the sons of gods and represented dharma, or cosmic order and balance, were on one side. The one hundred Kaurava brothers, representing disorder and chaos, were on the other. The battle for control of the kingdom constituted the main story line of the *Mahabharata*. In the end, the Pandava brothers won, but the five original brothers did not assume the throne but retreated to the Himalayas to meet final judgment for the part they played in the numerous battles—and the sin they still carry with them.

The epic, still taught to Indian schoolchildren today, is full of mythical beings, folktales, and philosophical digressions. But it is mainly a "warrior song," notes W. J. Johnson in his introduction to his translation of the tenth book of the *Mahābhārata, Massacre at Night*. He explains: "Like the Veda it was an oral composition, but purely heroic in character, dealing with legendary warrior heroes, and concerned with the warrior *dharma*, or code of conduct, and problems arising from its violation."[66] Krishna played a major role in helping the warriors on both sides to understand their duty to sacrifice and to act in accordance with the moral rules of conduct in war. In the Johnson translation of the *Massacre at Night*, Krishna explains this to the Kaurava son Asvatthaman:

In this world, the slaughter of the
sleeping

Is not respected as conforming to
dharma.

The same applies to those whose
arms have been laid down,

To those whose fighting chariots
have been unyoked,

To those who have declared their
allegiance,

To refugees, and those with
dishevelled hair,

To those, as well, whose chariots
have been destroyed. [67]

In this same passage, Krishna goes on
to explain what will happen if Asvatthaman violates this code:

Tonight, my lord, the Pāñcālas
[the opposing side] will sleep,

Their armour unbuckled, uncon-
scious as the dead,

All unsuspecting through the
dark till dawn.

The wicked man who seeks to
harm them in that state,

Without a doubt will dive into a
raftless,

Fathomless, shoreless hell. [68]

Asvatthaman, ignoring Krishna's words,
offered himself to the god of destruction,
Shiva. Shiva gave Asvatthaman a weapon
and then entered his body so that the warrior became "an embodiment of battle," [69]
according to the Johnson text. Thus
empowered, Asvatthaman fell into a killing
trance and was joined by demons who

"slaughtered [the sleeping warriors] as a
butcher slaughters" until hundreds were
dead and Asvatthaman was "triple-dyed in
blood." [70] This violation of the warrior code
brought even more destruction as the
demons were released from darkness and
ran about devouring flesh and drinking the
blood of the dead.

Krishna Explains Fate and the Warrior

The role of gods and fate is also examined
in the *Mahabharata.* In an earlier episode,
Arjuna, one of the five Pandava brothers,
has doubts about killing his own kin. He
questions Krishna in the most well known
scene from the epic, *The Bhagavad Gita,*
or the *Song of the Lord.* Krishna, in his role
as Arjuna's charioteer, has been by the
warrior's side throughout the battle.

In this passage of *The Bhagavad Gita,*
translated by Jack Hawley, Arjuna begins

Serpent Demons

*Serpent demons were common in Hindu
myth. Naga serpents had the body of a
snake and the head of a human. Anantas
serpents churned the earth's water. Both
serpents were associated with water.
Images of nagas and other demons were
often pictured in art and on the pillars of
shrines. Demons added much to the dra-
matic tension of myth, but they were also
seen as a complementary force in the
universe, a force of opposition that must
be dealt with to achieve balance.*

by acknowledging the power of Krishna. Arjuna tells the god that he is the "Imperishable Supreme Being, the one and only thing to be known. You are the ultimate refuge for all, the guardian and support for the universe. You are the very basis of the universe's functioning, what is called the Eternal *Dharma*. You are the everlasting Cosmic Spirit (*Purusha*)."[71]

However, this is the source of Arjuna's confusion. Why would a god with all this power allow war to happen? Arjuna tells Krishna,

I watch all the enemy forces—the sons of the old blind king, generals, heroes, relatives, others who allied themselves with them—all are rushing headlong into Your immensity as though being devoured. And I watch as vast numbers of our own soldiers and warrior-chiefs also rush heedless into the maw. I hear the frightful cries as these forces are ground up and crushed within You. Like flooded rivers rushing toward the ocean, the heroes on both sides are scurrying, stumbling to their awful fate in You; like moths flitting purposely into the flame, they rush to their doom in You. It is as though You are swallowing up the worlds and licking Your lips, O Lord. Your destructiveness is as a fierce blaze filling the sky, permeating the universe!"[72]

Arjuna demanded to know the purpose for all this destruction.

The warrior god Krishna drives the chariot of the warrior Arjuna into battle. Krishna promised Arjuna that fulfillment of his duty as a warrior would be rewarded in heaven.

The Path to Immortality

Thus, Krishna explains how a warrior's duty is to do his job without concern for the outcome. Duty and sacrifice are what mattered; the body was not the true self nor the eternal self. In Hawley's translation, Krishna's response is,

> I *am* Time, Arjuna—and now, here at this place of battle, I am the mighty world-destroying Time. With or without you, the warriors are arrayed to fight, and whether on the righteous or corrupt side, they are readied for their ruin and must die. The destruction of enemies is inevitable. It is not possible for an individual person to avert the design of Divinity. Therefore, attack, O mighty warrior, conquer your evil-doing enemies and win kingdom, wealth, and fame. I have willed to wipe out wickedness and have therefore already slain these warriors. Your actions will only be My outward cause, and you are merely My instrument. . . . they are already doomed.[73]

They continue their talk, with Krishna promising that faith in the divine order and the surrender to the will of the Supreme God will result in immortality.

In the final chapter of the epic, Krishna's words are proven to be true. The warrior Yudhisthera, the last of the Pandava brothers standing, finds both his own brothers and his cousins in heaven, all rewarded for doing their duty as warriors and for contributing to dharma. All is as it should be, as determined by the gods.

The myths of Hinduism are unique in that they have continued uninterrupted to modern times. Fighting in the Hindu myth always serves a clear purpose, as when the warrior gods and goddesses come to earth to protect or instruct. Additionally, warrior deities are a reminder that opposite forces such as evil and goodness, or order and chaos, are needed to achieve balance in the universe. The myths of Hinduism carry important spiritual messages for the people of both the past and the present.

The Hero Twins Fight the Forces of the Darkness

The Mayan civilization was located in what is now the Mexican states of Tabasco, Campeche, Chiapas, Quintana Roo, and the Yucatán, as well as parts of Guatemala, Belize, and Honduras. Artifacts from as early as 2000 B.C. illustrate the tenacity of this ancient agriculture-based culture—a culture that survive not only the challenging jungle environment but also many conflicts with neighboring tribes and outside invaders. The important Mayan centers had been in a state of decline for five hundred years when the Spanish arrived in the sixteenth century, and many more Maya died as a result of the Spanish Conquest; however, today 10 million Maya live in this region, observing the rituals and traditions of their ancestors.

Much of the mythology of the Maya was no doubt lost in the destruction by the Catholic missionaries who followed behind the Spanish conquerors in the sixteenth century. Thousands of written documents, called codices, and artifacts depicting Mayan deities were destroyed by the Catholic clergy. However, observes Timothy R. Roberts in *Gods of the Maya, Aztecs, and Incas*, "the Maya resisted the Spaniards for 180 years, defeated three Spanish armies, and even recruited Spanish renegades to help in the Maya fight for freedom."[74] This resistance, along with the impenetrability of their jungle cities, left many of the ruins virtually untouched.

When Mexico and Central America gained independence in 1810, researchers and explorers began to filter into this region. Mayan cities such as Copán, Mayapan, Tikal, Palenque, and Chichen Itzá were the subject of important archaeological discoveries. In the last 150 years, research into the Mayan civilization has revealed a complex culture.

The Mayan people had an elaborate writing system, a form of hieroglyphic texts which they carved into jade and stone or painted on pottery. Embedded in this ancient code are the Mayan calendar system and astronomical calculations, along with a record of historical rulers and other facts of history. Also, these ancient writings reveal key elements of Mayan myth. Fortunately, the *Popol Vuh*, a major source of Mayan myth from the Quiche region of Guatemala, was preserved and transcribed.

Mayan Area

YUCATÁN

Chichén Itzá

Mayapán

PUUC Hills

Tulúm

Gulf of Mexico

QUINTANA ROO

Bay of Campeche

CAMPECHE

M E X I C O

TABASCO

El Mirador

Uaxactun

Tikal

Palenque

BELIZE

Caribbean Sea

CHIAPAS

GUATEMALA

Copán

HONDURAS

Pacific Ocean

EL SALVADOR

A Prayer of Peace

In the *Popol Vuh,* translated by Dennis Tedlock, the great lords fasted, gave offerings to the gods, and prayed to the gods. Their prayer illustrates the desires of the Mayan people for a life of abundance and peace.

Wait! On this blessed day,
thou Hurricane, thou Heart of the Sky-Earth,
thou giver of ripeness and freshness,
and thou giver of daughters and sons,
spread thy stain, spill thy drops
of green and yellow;
give life and beginning
to those I bear and beget,
that they might multiply and grow,
nurturing and providing for thee,
calling to thee along the roads and paths,
on rivers, in canyons,
beneath the trees and bushes;
give them their daughters and sons.

May there be no blame, obstacle, want, or misery;
let no deceiver come behind or before them,
may they neither be snared nor wounded,
nor seduced, nor burned,
nor diverted below the road nor above it;
may they neither fall over backward nor stumble;
keep them on the Green Road, the Green Path.

May there be no blame or barrier for them
through any secrets or sorcery of thine;
may thy nurturers and providers be good
before thy mouth and thy face;
thou, Heart of Sky; thou, Heart of Earth;
thou, Bundle of Flames;
and thou, Tohil, Auilix, Hacauitz,
under the sky, on the earth,
the four sides, the four corners;
may there be only light, only continuity within,
before thy mouth and thy face, thou god.

Mayans and War

From such artifacts and uncovered ruins, scholars now know that the Maya, who lived in city-states and fought among themselves, participated in war and war rituals involving their gods. Murals recovered from ancient sites depict warriors armed with spears, slingshots, and shields and engaged in gruesome scenes of torture and decapitation. The Maya believed that their gods were pleased with their bloody rituals of war. Notes writer Roberts in *Gods of the Maya, Aztecs, and Incas*, the Maya "adopted the sacrificial customs of the Aztecs and sacrificed war captives by stretching them backward over a stone atop one of the great pyramids, slicing their chests open, and tearing the still-beating hearts out with their hands."[75] While some of these depictions may have been propaganda, artifacts from graves support these Mayan rituals.

Violent scenes of war are at the heart of the Mayan myth. The Maya divided their universe into three spheres: the Upperworld, the Underworld, and the Middleworld. A key image of the Mayan myth was a turtle. Below it was the watery Underworld. The turtle's back represented Earth, or the Middleworld, which was shared by both the Upperworld and the Underworld. The Upperworld included gods of the sky and, according to Lynn V. Foster in *Handbook to Life in the Ancient Maya World*, "served as a stage upon which the actions of the gods were played out."[76] The planet Venus had particular significance for the Maya. "The Maya associated Venus with war and regard-ed its presence as powerful and its influences potentially dangerous. Rulers timed military campaigns according to the appearances of Venus,"[77] notes Foster.

The Maya believed that all forms of nature were imbued with a spirit or sacredness called *k'ul* and deities or gods were in control of the universe. Explains Foster,

> In ancient Maya thought, the universe was suffused with sacredness that resonated from the presence of deities. The ancestors, spirits, and deities not only resided in the Upperworld and the Underworld, but also shared the Middleworld, or Earth, with its human and animal populations. In the Middleworld, supernatural beings claimed extraordinary geological features of the natural landscape as their special precincts and magnetized architectural structures that humans constructed for ritual purposes.[78]

Thus, the Maya attributed special significance to such landforms as mountains and caves, and the structures they built at their centers, such as temples and underground tombs, were a means of connecting with their gods.

Mayan Gods of Power

The most powerful god of the Maya was Itzamná, creator of the universe. Itzamná was presented in Mayan myth in many forms. Most commonly, Itzamná took the form of a sun's disc and was credited with teaching the Maya how to grow corn. He was also a bird, sometimes portrayed as Principal Bird Deity, Itzam-Ye, or Vuqub Caquix. As the Milky Way, he appeared as a two-headed reptile or serpent. As the serpent of the Milky Way, his body was the sky, his front head was the eastern rising sun, and his rear head was the western setting sun or Venus, the evening star.

Another significant god was the god of the sun, K'inich Ahaw. Interestingly, as the sun god, he crossed the sky during the day, but at night, he transformed into a jaguar and became a war deity of the Underworld. K'inich Ahaw is featured on the Temple of the Sun, a relief tablet found at Palenque. The tablet pictures the shield

An eighth-century sculpture found in Honduras depicts the god Itzamná, the creator of the universe in Mayan mythology.

The Mayans used a stone calendar like this one to track the movements of the visible planets, which they revered as manifestations of the gods.

of the Jaguar God of the Underworld, with crossed spears, death darts, and war captives.

Sometimes the god Chak is said to be a war god. Chak, portrayed as a reptile with scales and catfishlike whiskers, is a rain deity who, like other storm gods in other cultures, wields his power with lightning and thunderbolts. In some imagery, Chak is seen holding stone axes and powerful serpents. Chak, like other Mesoamerican gods, had a four-part identity and was associated with the four directions and four colors. He was powerful but also a god of benevolence, and farmers knew to appeal to him for rain.

The ancient book of the *Popol Vuh*, using a combination of words and pic-

tures, illustrates the impact these gods, and others, had on the world of humans. The *Popol Vuh* begins, as do many creation myths, with the original gods, the Sovereign Plumed Serpent and Heart of Sky, shaping the world, or "sky-earth" as they called it, and putting the sun and moon, and the earth and sky in their proper places. To accomplish this, the gods of the primordial sky descended to a water-covered earth that was ruled by the gods of the primordial seas. Together they decided that land would emerge from the water and on it crops would grow. As Foster points out, the gods took this new sky-earth and "measured its sides and corners with cords, an action parallel to those of Maya farmers when they prepare their

A painting by famed Mexican artist Diego Rivera reproduces the creation of the earth as depicted in the *Popol Vuh*, *a collection of Mayan myths*.

maize field with measuring cords."[79] With the four corners of the earth squared off, the gods produced animals, forests, canyons, and mountains. They separated the waters, putting rivers and seas in their place. But there was nothing on earth to worship the gods, so the Plumed Serpent of the earth and the Heart of Sky decided to make humans.

The Creation and Destruction of Humans

The making of a suitable human was no easy feat, and the gods had no qualms about destroying inferior models. The first being was constructed out of clay, but this material did not hold up to the challenges of being human. The gods destroyed it

and tried again, this time working with wood. But this race of wooden people, writes Karl Taube in *Aztec and Maya Myths*, were "dry, bloodless beings with expressionless faces. The wooden people lack souls and understanding, and do not respect or worship their creators."[80] To rid the world of their mistake, the creator gods brought on a great flood that crushed the world and demolished the wooden people.

Dennis Tedlock describes the destruction in his recently revised translation of *Popol Vuh*:

> And so they were killed, done in
> by a flood:
> There came a rain of resin from
> the sky.

There came the one named
Gouger of Faces: he gouged out
their eyeballs.

There came Sudden Bloodletter:
he snapped off their heads.

There came Crunching Jaguar:
he ate their flesh.

There came Tearing Tiger: he
tore them open.

They were pounded down to the
bones and tendons, smashed
and pulverized even to the
bones. Their faces were
smashed because they were
incompetent before their mother and father, the Heart of Sky,
named Hurricane.[81]

Hero Twins and the Underworld, Xibalba

The *Popol Vuh* then turns to the adventures of the Hero Twins. It is up to the
Hero Twins to help prepare the world for
the next set of humans. To do so, they
must journey to the Underworld, also
called Xibalba or Place of Fear, to face the
demons of darkness. This conflict is at the
heart of the *Popol Vuh* myth. If the twins
succeed in defeating the gods of the dark,
the gods can proceed with the creation of
humans on earth.

In fact, there are two sets of Hero Twins
in the *Popol Vuh*. Their adventures are
related in reverse order, with the younger
set of twins entering the story first and
then the older set presented later, in flash-
back fashion. Both sets of twins, howev-

er, are needed to successfully battle the
forces of the Underworld. The older set of
twins are the brothers One Hunahpu and
Seven Hunahpu. The younger set of twins
is Hunahpu and Xbalanque, sons of One
Hunahpu and Blood Moon, the daughter
of an Underworld god named Blood
Gatherer.

In the true sequence of events, the conflict begins with the older Hero Twins,
One Hunahpu and Seven Hunahpu, who
disturbed the gods of the Underworld by
their noisy playing of the Mayan ball game
(a popular sport somewhat like a cross
between basketball and soccer). The noise
generated by the ball on the clay court so
annoyed the gods of the dark that the
twins were summoned by the monster owls
to come to the Underworld ball court.

The trip to Xibalba was filled with dangerous trials and tests set up by the gods.
The first test for One Hunahpu and Seven
Hunahpu was to pass through treacher-
ous canyons and Scorpion Rapids that
were filled with stinging scorpions. Their
next obstacle was Blood River and after
that a river filled with pus. The twins
finally arrived in Xibalba, only to be
offered a seat on a burning hot bench.

Death in the Dark House

The next trial was even more challenging. The twins were placed for the night
in a Dark House, where there was no light
at all. The twins were handed a torch and
two cigars, but were told that in the morning, the cigars must not be touched in any
way, or the twins would both be sacrificed.

Of course, in a house as dark as that one, the twins lit the torch and smoked the cigars, so in the morning, they faced their death. Their bodies were buried in the Place of Ball Game Sacrifice, and the head of one of the twins, One Hunahpu, was hung from a nearby tree.

Magical things began to happen with this severed head. For the first time, this tree bore fruit, and the head of One Hunahpu looked so much like the fruit that no one could see it anymore. Writes Tedlock, "This is the origin of the calabash tree, whose fruit has the character of a human skull when dried and hollowed."[82] An Underworld maiden, Blood Moon, came by, eager to taste the fruit. She reached for the fruit that was, in fact, One Hunahpu's head. Alarmed by her

The Deadly Ball Game

Like the Hero Twins, the Maya played a ball game that had high stakes: The losers were decapitated as an offering to the gods. More of a ceremonial ritual than a game of sport, the ball game was played on a court between stone walls. Using only their elbows and hips, the players had to knock a rubber ball through stone hoops on either end of the court. The Mayan word for "court" is hom. Some scholars suggest that it was no coincidence that this was also the word for graveyard, as the game had such severe consequences for the losers.

actions, One Hunahpu warned her not to touch, spitting on her hand to dissuade her. The saliva was more than a warning, however. It would make the maiden pregnant with his child.

Her father, an Underworld lord named Blood Gatherer, was not pleased when he discovered that his daughter was pregnant. He ordered her killed. The same monster owls who came for the twins on earth were sent to kill Blood Moon, with orders to return with her heart. But Blood Moon was persuasive, and she convinced them that instead of taking her heart back to her father, to take instead a glob of bloody sap from the calabash tree. This did indeed fool the father of Blood Moon, and the young woman was able to flee out of the Underworld and up to earth. Blood Moon found the mother of One Hunahpu and told the old woman that she, Blood Moon, was about to give birth to One Hunahpu's child. To prove herself, Blood Moon was sent by the old woman out to the fields, from which she was to return with an armful of corn. She did so, miraculously producing many ears from the silk of one ear. The old woman knew that Blood Moon was telling the truth.

Hunahpu and Xbalanque

Blood Moon gave birth to a second set of twins, the Hero Twins Hunahpu and Xbalanque. These twins were not welcomed by the family, particularly by their half brothers, One Monkey and One Artisan, who were the sons One Hunahpu

Constantly agonized by their half brothers, the Hero Twins of Mayan myth spent much of their time hunting birds with a blowgun, as depicted on this Guatemalan vase.

had left behind. One Monkey and One Artisan were jealous and angry. To avoid the unpleasantness of their half brothers and their grandmother who gave them no love, the twins spent their days shooting their blowguns and killing birds for the family.

Finally the Hero Twins decided to get rid of their half brothers. One day they came home and told their grandmother that they had killed some birds, but the birds were hung up in a tree and they needed their older brothers to help them get the birds down. This was a trick, of course, but One Monkey and One Artisan did not realize it. Instead they climbed the tree, and once they were high in the branches, the tree grew taller and the trunk grew thicker. The boys were stranded there. In one version of this part of the myth, the grandmother Xmucane could not help but laugh at their plight. Wounded by their grandmother's slight, the two brothers remained as monkeys in the tree for the rest of their lives.

The twins, freed from their annoying brothers, decided to clear a ball game court in the jungle. When they began to play, they, like their father and uncle, disturbed the gods below. Once again, the Hero Twins were summoned to Xibalba. Before they left, they planted a stalk of corn in the front of the house, telling their grandmother not to touch it until their return. If the corn did not resprout in the spring, she would know they had died in the Underworld.

Underworld Trials for the Younger Hero Twins

Like their father and uncle before them, the Hero Twins knew their trip to the Underworld would be dangerous, but they were determined not to fail the tests their father and uncle were given. For example, when they got to the Dark House, they knew not to burn the cigars, but instead put fireflies on the cigar tips. Thus, they were not sacrificed as their father was, but survived long enough to engage in the serious ball game with the gods.

Hunahpu and Xbalanque were on their guard as their game began. The lords of the dark used a ball that was not a ball at all, but a skull. When Hunahpu hit it, it fell apart and a dagger fell out of it. Fortunately, the twins were able to avoid being hit by the dagger as it chased them on the court. In the next game, the twins

used their own ball. The lord of Xibalba agreed that instead of death, the winner must provide the loser with four bowls of flowers. The twins lost and had a day to come up with bunches of flowers to give to their opponents.

The Razor House and Other Challenges

That night they were put in the Razor House, a place where free-swinging blades cut at will. The twins made a deal with the blades, promising that if they stoped cutting for the night, animals would be provided for them as food. The blades ceased, and the twins were free to hunt for the flowers that they needed to have in their possession by the morning. To do so, they engaged leaf-cutting ants, who with ease cut all the flowers the brothers needed.

After this, they were locked in the Cold House, where falling ice chunks almost killed them, and then in the Jaguar House, home of hungry jaguars. The toughest house of all, the Bat House, was full of flying bats that were so intimidating that the twins took shelter in their blowguns. But when Hunahpu popped his head out of the blowgun to look around, one of the bats took his head off. Like his father before him, Hunahpu was killed and his head was to be used as the ball on the ball court. When Xbalanque discovered this, he tried to help out his brother. Quickly he replaced Hunahpu's head, planting a squash on his shoulders.

With his new squash head, Hunahpu was ready to play ball. As they began to play, the twin's original head came rolling into the court. Xbalanque grabbed it, put it back on Hunahpu's shoulders, then retrieved the squash and proceeded to play. The dark gods of the Xibalba had not seen any of this, but when the squash exploded on the court, they knew they had been tricked.

The Rising of the Sun

The final challenge of the Hero Twins was the most complicated of all. The twins knew that the gods were determined to kill them, so they solicited the help of two seers named Xulu and Pacam who told the twins how to escape death. When the time came for the next trial, and the gods challenged the twins to a contest that involved jumping over a burning pit, the twins surprised them by jumping directly into it. Delighted, the gods of Xibalba crushed their bones and threw them into the river. After five days, the Hero Twins appeared first as catfish, and then as

Lords of the Underworld

The lords of the Underworld, One and Seven Death, are very clear about the assigned duties of the Underworld demons. This translation is from Dennis Tedlock's *Popol Vuh.*

And these are the lords over everything; each lord with a commission and a domain assigned by One and Seven Death:

There are the lords named Scab Stripper and Blood Gatherer. And this is their commission; to draw blood from people.

Next are the lordships of Demon of Pus and Demon of Jaundice. And this is their domain: to make people swell up, to make pus come out of their legs, to make their faces yellow, to cause jaundice. . . .

Next are the lords of Bone Scepter and Skull Scepter, the staff bearers of Xibalba; their staffs are just bones. And this is their staff-bearing: to reduce people to bones, right down to the bones and skulls, until they die from emaciation and edema. . . .

Next are the lords named Demon of Filth and Demon of Woe. This is their commission: just to give people a sudden fright whenever they have filth or grime in the doorway of the house, the patio of the house. Then they're struck, they're just punctured till they crawl on the ground, then die. . . .

Next are the lords named Wing and Packstrap. This is their domain: that people should die in the road, just "sudden death," as it is called. Blood comes to the mouth, then there is death from vomiting blood. So to each of them his burden, the load on his shoulders: just to strike people on the neck and chest. Then there is death in the road, and then they just go on causing suffering, whether one is coming or going.

humans in disguise. In an elaborate act of illusion, the disguised twins staged a performance for the gods in which they burned down a house but did so without killing the inhabitant. In the great finale of the show they put on, Xbalanque killed Hunahpu, took off his head, cut out his heart, and then brought him back to life. The gods were tremendously impressed and begged to be a part of the act. The Hero Twins agreed, but of course they actually killed the gods.

Now in a position of power, the Hero Twins told the monsters and gods of the Underworld that sacrifices of humans were no longer allowed and that attacks on humans should cease. Then the twins returned to the court, where the head and

body of their uncle, Seven Hunahpu, was still buried. As he could not speak, they had to leave him there, but they declared that one day a year would be set aside in his name, Hunahpu, to honor the dead. This is one of the oldest traditions of the Maya and still continues today.

The job of the Hero Twins was done and they took their place in the sky, bringing light to the earth. According to the Tedlock translation of the *Popul Vuh*, "The two boys ascended this way, here into the middle of the light, and they ascended straight on into the sky, and the sun belongs to one and the moon to the other. When it became light within the sky, on the face of the earth, they were there in the sky."[83] There they were joined by hundreds of stars.

This Diego Rivera painting depicts the creation of man in the Popol Vuh. *After the Hero Twins ascended into the heavens, the Mayan gods were free to create the first human.*

Good People, an Orderly World

With the coming of light, the gods were free to create the first human. The grandmother of the Hero Twins was instrumental in making this happen. When she mixed a paste of corn, the first beings of a new race of humans were formed. This race had everything the others did not, including the ability to worship the gods that created them.

In fact, they were too perfect. They could see all of the universe, just as the gods could. They were simply too godlike. According to Tedlock's *Popol Vuh*:

They were good people, handsome, with looks of the male kind. Thoughts came into existence and they gazed; their vision came all at once. Perfectly they saw, perfectly they knew everything under the sky, whenever they looked. The moment they turned around and looked around in the sky, on the earth, everything was seen without obstruction. They didn't have to walk around before they could see what was under the sky; they just stayed where they were. [84]

The gods were afraid the people would become their equals. Something needed to be done. The gods decided to throw a mist over the humans' eyes so that their vision was fuzzy. In their flawed state, the four humans were each given wives. From these people, the Quiche were born. They spread throughout the region, forming different groups of peoples who spoke different languages and worshiped all the great gods.

With the tribes spread across the world, the orderly rhythm of the universe fell into place. For every tribe, a dawn appeared. The sun rose in the sky and dried out the earth. Each day it followed an orderly path across the sky. The humans organized themselves by a calendar with the movement of the sky and the planets. Maize grew, human beings peopled the earth, and creation was complete.

The myths of the Maya, as seen through the *Popol Vuh*, along with the other remnants of myth in pottery and writings, offer a vivid portrayal of a people who used tales of fighting to explain the formation of their earth and skies and the rhythmic patterns of the universe. They believed that their world was created through a series of battles between the gods of the sky and the gods of Xibalba. The defeat of the gods of darkness brought forth the sun and the stars and the predictable cycles of the earth that allowed crops to grow and people to prosper.

Notes

Introduction: Mythical Worlds of Conflict and Peace

1. Charles Freeman, *The Greek Achievement: The Foundation of the Western World.* New York: Viking, 1999, p. 62.

Chapter One: Ancient Battles Between the Babylonian Gods of Creation

2. Stephanie Dalley, trans., *Myths from Mesopotamia: Creation, the Flood, Gilgamesh, and Others.* Oxford: Oxford University Press, 1989, p. 234.
3. Tamra Andrews, *Dictionary of Nature Myths: Legends of the Earth, Sea, and Sky.* Oxford: Oxford University Press, 1998, p. 204.
4. John Gray, *Near Eastern Mythology.* New York: Peter Bedrick Books, 1982, p. 33.
5. Dalley, *Myths from Mesopotamia,* p. 249.
6. Gray, *Near Eastern Mythology,* p. 35.
7. Gray, *Near Eastern Mythology,* p. 35.
8. Stephen Bertman, *Handbook to Life in Ancient Mesopotamia.* New York: Facts On File, 2003, p. 64.
9. N.K. Sandars, trans., *The Epic of Gilgamesh.* London: Penguin Books, 1972, p. 61.
10. Sandars, *The Epic of Gilgamesh,* p. 71.
11. Sandars, *The Epic of Gilgamesh,* p. 81.
12. Sandars, *The Epic of Gilgamesh,* p. 89.
13. Dalley, *Myths from Mesopotamia,* p. 208.
14. Dalley, *Myths from Mesopotamia,* p. 215.
15. Dalley, *Myths from Mesopotamia,* p. 218.

Chapter Two: Power Struggles in the Aegean

16. Robert Fagles, trans., *Homer: The Iliad.* New York: Viking, 1990, p. 24.
17. M.L. West, trans., *Hesiod: Theogony* and *Works and Days.* Oxford: Oxford University Press, 1999, p. 22.
18. West, *Hesiod: Theogony,* p. 27.
19. Félix Guirand, *Greek Mythology.* London: Paul Hamlyn, 1963, p. 22.
20. Ellen Switzer, *Greek Myths: Gods, Heroes and Monsters: Their Sources, Their Stories and Their Meanings.* New York: Atheneum, 1988, p. 20.
21. Freeman, *The Greek Achievement,* p. 46.
22. Fagles, *Homer: The Iliad,* p. 33.
23. Fagles, *Homer: The Iliad,* p. 210.
24. Fagles, *Homer: The Iliad,* p. 310.
25. Fagles, *Homer: The Iliad,* p. 26.
26. W.H.D. Rouse, trans., *Homer: The Iliad: The Story of Achilles.* New York: Signet Classic, 1999, p. 200.
27. Rouse, *Homer,* p. 201.
28. Fagles *Homer: The Iliad,* p. 604.
29. Fagles, *Homer: The Iliad,* p. 605.
30. Fagles, *Homer: The Iliad,* p. 43.

Chapter Three: Warrior Magic

31. Anne Ross, *The Pagan Celts.* London: B.T. Batsford, 1986, p. 40.
32. Thomas Kinsella, trans., *The Tain.* Philadelphia: University of Pennsylvania Press, 1985, pp. 195–96.
33. Timothy R. Roberts, *The Celts in Myth and Legend.* New York: MetroBooks, 1995, p. 37.
34. Anne Ross, *Druids, Gods, and Heroes from Celtic Mythology.* New York: Schocken Books 1986, p. 17.
35. Proinsias Mac Cana, *Celtic Mythology.* New York: Peter Bedrick Books, 1985, p. 58.
36. Mac Cana, *Celtic Mythology,* p. 58.

37. Miranda J. Green, *Dictionary of Celtic Myth and Legend.* London: Thames and Hudson, 1992, p. 216.

38. Mac Cana, *Celtic Mythology*, pp. 104–105.

39. Green, *Dictionary of Celtic Myth and Legend*, p. 70.

40. Kinsella, *The Tain*, p. 77.

41. Roberts, *The Celts in Myth and Legend*, p. 57.

42. Ross, *The Pagan Celts*, p. 10.

43. Roberts, *The Celts in Myth and Legend*, p. 51.

44. Miranda J. Green, *Celtic Myths.* Austin: University of Texas Press, 1993, p. 24.

45. Kinsella, *The Tain*, p. 253.

Chapter Four: War and Peace in the Wild Land of the Giants

46. H.A. Guerber, *Myths of the Norsemen from the Eddas and Sagas.* London: George G. Harrap, 1908, p. 4.

47. Kevin Crossley-Holland, *The Norse Myths.* New York: Pantheon Books, 1980, p. 4.

48. P. Grappin, "Germanic Lands: The Mortal Gods," in ed. Pierre Grimal, *Larousse World Mythology.* London: Paul Hamlyn, 1971, p. 365.

49. Guerber, *Myths of the Norsemen*, pp. 16–17.

50. Guerber, *Myths of the Norsemen*, p. 19.

51. Crossley-Holland, *The Norse Myths*, p. 93.

52. H.R. Ellis Davidson, *Scandinavian Mythology.* New York: Paul Hamlyn, 1969, p. 52.

53. Peter Andreas Munch, *Norse Mythology: Legends of Gods and Heroes.* New York: American-Scandinavian Foundation, 1942, p. 23.

54. Guerber, *Myths of the Norsemen*, p. 197.

55. Munch, *Norse Mythology*, p. 109.

56. Munch, *Norse Mythology*, p. 109.

57. Guerber, *Myths of the Norsemen*, p. 334.

58. Grappin, "Germanic Lands: The Mortal Gods," p. 397.

59. Guerber, *Myths of the Norsemen*, p. 337.

Chapter Five: Vishnu and Other Demon-Fighters of Hindu Myth

60. Veronica Ions, *Indian Mythology.* New York: Peter Bedrick Books, 1984, p. 17.

61. Ions, *Indian Mythology*, pp. 18–19.

62. Ions, *Indian Mythology*, p. 89.

63. Ions, *Indian Mythology*, p. 89.

64. Wendy Doniger O'Flaherty, *Hindu Myths: A Sourcebook Translated from the Sanskrit.* London: Penguin Books, 1975, p. 179.

65. Ions, *Indian Mythology*, p. 53.

66. W.J. Johnson, trans., *The Sauptikaparvan of the Mahābhārata: The Massacre at Night.* Oxford: Oxford University Press, 1998, p. xvi.

67. Johnson, *The Sauptikaparvan*, p. 22.

68. Johnson, *The Sauptikaparvan*, p. 22.

69. Johnson, *The Sauptikaparvan*, p. 33.

70. Johnson, *The Sauptikaparvan*, p. 37.

71. Jack Hawley, trans., *The Bhagavad Gita: A Walkthrough for Westerners.* Novato, CA: New World Library, 2001, pp. 101–102.

72. Hawley, *The Bhagavad Gita*, p. 103.

73. Hawley, *The Bhagavad Gita*, pp. 103–104.

Chapter Six: The Hero Twins Fight the Forces of the Darkness

74. Timothy R. Roberts, *Gods of the Maya, Aztecs, and Incas.* New York: MetroBooks, 1996, p. 16.

75. Roberts, *Gods of the Maya, Aztecs, and Incas*, p. 18.

76. Lynn V. Foster, *Handbook to Life in the Ancient Maya World*. New York: Facts On File, 2002, p. 161.

77. Foster, *Handbook to Life in the Ancient Maya World*, p. 161.

78. Foster, *Handbook to Life in the Ancient Maya World*, p. 159.

79. Foster, *Handbook to Life in the Ancient Maya World*, p. 183.

80. Karl Taube, *Aztec and Maya Myths*. Austin: University of Texas Press, 1993, p. 55.

81. Dennis Tedlock, trans., *Popol Vuh: The Mayan Book of the Dawn of Life*. Rev. ed. New York: Simon & Schuster, 1996, p. 71.

82. Tedlock, *Popol Vuh*, p. 36.

83. Tedlock, *Popol Vuh*, p. 141.

84. Tedlock, *Popol Vuh*, p. 147.

For Further Reading

Books

Victor Montejo, *Popol Vuh: A Sacred Book of the Maya*. Toronto, Ontario: Groundwood Books, 1999. A readable telling of this ancient Mayan myth, with full-page illustrations of story scenes.

Anne Ross, *Druids, Gods, and Heroes from Celtic Mythology*. New York: Schocken Books, 1986. A highly readable collection of tales with drawings to illustrate the story.

Madhu Bazaz Wangu, *Hinduism*. New York: Facts On File, 2001. A very readable introduction to Hinduism from ancient to modern times.

Philip Wilkinson, *Illustrated Dictionary of Mythology: Heroes, Heroines, Gods, and Goddesses from Around the World*. New York: DK, 1998. Beautiful artwork augments this introduction to world myths.

Web Sites

Encyclopedia Mythica: An Encyclopedia on Mythology, Folklore, and Legend (www.pantheon.org). A good source for quick reference of myths from around the world. Includes thousands of definitions of major figures, some images, and links to other sites.

Greek Mythology (http://homepage.mac.com/cparada/GML/index.html). This Web site, created and maintained by Danish genealogist Carlos Parada, is an excellent source for referencing people and events in Greek myth. Maps and art are excellent supplements to the text.

Táin Bó Cúalinge (http:/vassun.vassar.edu/~sttaylor/Cooley). Compiled by Steve Taylor, this is an adaptation of the Joseph Dunn translation of an epic of the Ulster cycle of Celtic myth. The epic is divided nicely into episodes, making the text easy to navigate.

Works Consulted

Tamra Andrews, *Dictionary of Nature Myths: Legends of the Earth, Sea, and Sky*. Oxford: Oxford University Press, 1998. This wonderful resource covers all types of myths relating to the natural world.

Stephen Bertman, *Handbook to Life in Ancient Mesopotamia*. New York: Facts On File, 2003. Covers the basics of ancient Mesopotamia from geography to government to religion.

Kevin Crossley-Holland, *The Norse Myths*. New York: Pantheon Books, 1980. A collection of thirty-two Norse tales, told in a highly readable, entertaining style. The map of the nine worlds of Norse myth is useful.

Stephanie Dalley, trans., *Myths from Mesopotamia: Creation, the Flood, Gilgamesh, and Others*. Oxford: Oxford University Press, 1989. An excellent translation of the important myths from this ancient region. Includes a useful map and glossary.

H.R. Ellis Davidson, *Scandinavian Mythology*. New York: Paul Hamlyn, 1969. A thorough exploration of all the facets of Norse myth, beginning with the earliest evidence of gods in the northern cultures. Text and accompanying photographs emphasize artwork and other archaeological findings in support of theories of early god and goddess worship.

Robert Fagles, trans., *Homer: The Iliad*. New York: Viking, 1990. A wonderfully readable translation of Homer's epic, with information, introduction, and endnotes by Harvard scholar Bernard Knox.

Anthony Faulkes, trans., *Snorri Sturluson Edda*. London: J.M. Dent, 1987. A very readable translation of Sturluson's *Prose Edda*.

Lynn V. Foster, *Handbook to Life in the Ancient Maya World*. New York: Facts On File, 2002. An excellent up-to-date overview of Mayan life.

Charles Freeman, *The Greek Achievement: The Foundation of the Western World*. New York: Viking, 1999. An excellent discussion of current and past approaches to the lasting achievements of the Greeks.

John Gray, *Near Eastern Mythology*. New York: Peter Bedrick Books, 1982. Part of the Library of the World's Myths and Legends, this book covers the principal myths of Mesopotamia, Canaan, and Israel.

Miranda J. Green, *Celtic Myths*. Austin: University of Texas Press, 1993. Part of the Legendary Past series, this thin book succinctly covers major components of Celtic myth, with an emphasis on archaeology and sources. Photos of artwork supplement.

———, *Dictionary of Celtic Myth and Legend*. London: Thames and Hudson, 1992. An excellent resource on figures and concepts of Celtic myth; includes photographs and drawings of artifacts and figures.

Pierre Grimal, ed., *Larousse World Mythology*. New York: Paul Hamlyn, 1971. A comprehensive study of mythologies of the world, with photos of mythical figures and artwork.

H.A. Guerber, *Myths of the Norsemen from the Eddas and Sagas*. London: George G. Harrap, 1908. This old collection of myths is a treasure. Chapters tell the tales of all the major gods, supplemented by original poetry from original sources. Includes exquisite color illustrations of story scenes.

Félix Guirand, *Greek Mythology*. London: Paul Hamlyn, 1963. A very clearly written text that covers all the significant gods and heroes of Greek myth. Well-placed photos of ruins, sculptures, and other art.

Jack Hawley, trans., *The Bhagavad Gita: A Walkthrough for Westerners*. Novato, CA: New World Library, 2001. This epic poem is presented here in a very accessible prose version that captures the spirit of the ancient text.

Veronica Ions, *Indian Mythology*. New York: Peter Bedrick Books, 1984. Part of the excellent Library of the World's Myths and Legends, this illustrated text covers thoroughly all aspects of Indian mythology, including Vedic, Hindu, Buddhist, and Jain.

W.J. Johnson, trans., *The Sauptikaparvan of the Mahābhārata: The Massacre at Night*. Oxford: Oxford University Press, 1998. A riveting translation of Kaurava warrior Asvatthaman's massacre of the Pandavas while they sleep. Included are an introduction and summary of the complete epic.

Brian P. Katz, *Deities and Demons of the Far East*. New York: MetroBooks, 1995. Colorful photographs and sketches accompany this overview of Indian mythology. Japanese and Chinese mythology are covered as well.

Thomas Kinsella, trans., *The Táin*. Philadelphia: University of Pennsylvania Press, 1985. An intriguing translation of the Irish *Táin Bó Cuailnge* from the Ulster cycle. Text is illustrated by Louis Le Brocquy, with black ink brush drawings.

Carolyne Larrington, trans., *The Poetic Edda*. New York: Oxford University Press, 1996. A very readable collection of Norse and Icelandic poetry.

Richmond Lattimore, trans., *The Iliad of Homer*. Chicago: University of Chicago Press, 1951. A classic translation of Homer's epic.

C. Scott Littleton, ed., *The Sacred East: An Illustrated Guide to Buddhism, Hinduism, Confucianism, Taoism, and Shintoism*. Berkeley, CA: Ulysses Press, 1999. The chapter on Hinduism, written by Professor Mary McGee, ties ancient myths to modern practices. Photos and clear explanations make this a very accessible text.

Proinsias Mac Cana, *Celtic Mythology*. New York: Peter Bedrick Books, 1985. Part of the Library of the World's Myths and Legends, this is an excellent overview of all aspects of Celtic myth, with abundant photographs of art and artifacts.

Henrietta McCall, *Mesopotamian Myths*. Austin: University of Texas Press, 1990. McCall relies on quoted lines from original texts to tell the key myths of Mesopotamia. Photos and sketches illustrate.

Anthony S. Mercatante, *The Facts On File Encyclopedia of World Mythology and Legend*. New York: Facts On File, 1988. Readable entries, some in story form, and an annotated bibliography organized by culture make this a valuable resource.

Peter Andreas Munch, *Norse Mythology: Legends of Gods and Heroes*. New York: American-Scandinavian Foundation, 1942. This classic collection covers descriptions of all the mythic figures and the most popular tales.

Wendy Doniger O'Flaherty, *Hindu Myths: A Sourcebook Translated from the Sanskrit*. London: Penguin Books, 1975. Excerpts from all major Hindu and Vedic works, organized by major gods.

John Pinsent, *Greek Mythology*. New York: Peter Bedrick Books, 1983. Another in the Library of the World's Myths and Legends, this is an excellent overview of all aspects of Greek myth, with abundant photographs of art and artifacts.

Kay Almere Read and Jason J. Gonzalez, *Handbook of Mesoamerican Mythology*. Santa Barbara, CA: ABC-CLIO, 2000. Detailed descriptions and explanations of gods and concepts of Mesoamerican myth. Includes an annotated bibliography of books, videos, and Web sites.

Timothy R. Roberts, *The Celts in Myth and Legend*. New York: MetroBooks, 1995. This introduction to Celtic myth is accompanied by beautiful photographs of the land and ancient sculptures and artifacts.

————, *Gods of the Maya, Aztecs, and Incas*. New York: MetroBooks, 1996. Beautifully illustrated introduction to these three cultures.

Anne Ross, *The Pagan Celts*. London: B.T. Batsford, 1986. A well-presented overview of the Celtic world, with lots of interesting details and helpful drawings and photos.

W.H.D. Rouse, trans., *Homer: The Iliad: The Story of Achilles*. New York: Signet Classic, 1999. Rouse captures the language of Homer in this readable prose version of the epic.

N.K. Sandars, trans., *The Epic of Gilgamesh*. London: Penguin Books, 1972. This prose translation includes a helpful, informative introduction.

Robert J. Sharer, *Daily Life in Maya Civilization*. Westport, CT: Greenwood Press, 1996. A thorough look at Mayan life, including myth, art, government, and economics.

Ellen Switzer, *Greek Myths: Gods, Heroes and Monsters: Their Sources, Their Stories and Their Meanings*. New York: Atheneum, 1988. Good source of information on both myth and the culture that produced it. Photographs by Costas accompany the highly readable text.

Karl Taube, *Aztec and Maya Myths*. Austin: University of Texas Press, 1993. Part of the Legendary Past series, this thin book provides a good introduction to Mayan myth, with an emphasis on recent archaeological findings and interpretations.

Dennis Tedlock, trans., *Popol Vuh: The Mayan Book of the Dawn of Life*. Rev. ed. New York: Simon & Schuster, 1996. A splendid translation of the Mayan creation myth, with Mayan drawings to illustrate the story.

M.L. West, trans., *Hesiod: Theogony* and *Works and Days*. Oxford: Oxford University Press, 1999. A delightful translation of these two short works.

Index

Picture Credits

About the Author

This is Susan Glick's second book in the Discovering Mythology series. *The Natural World* was published in fall 2003. Ms. Glick, who has a master's degree in English language and literature from the University of Maryland, has taught writing to students of all levels, from elementary school to college. Currently she works with high school students who have learning disabilities. Ms. Glick is the author of *One Shot*, a novel for young adults.